CHRISTMAS POEMS

BARNES & NOBLE POETRY LIBRARY

CHRISTMAS POEMS

LOVE POEMS

POEMS OF FUN AND FANCY

POEMS OF THE AMERICAN SPIRIT

POEMS OF VISION AND PROPHECY

CHRISTMAS POEMS

SERIES EDITOR
DAVID STANFORD BURR

BARNES & NOBLE POETRY LIBRARY

2002 Barnes & Noble Books

ISBN 0-7607-3310-4

Text design by Rhea Braunstein

Printed and bound in the United States of America

02 03 04 05 M 9 8 7 6 5 4 3 2 1

RRD-C

Contents

CONTENTS

Foreword

Christmas Poems is a poetic holiday offering that recaptures the mystery and fun not only of a single day, but of an entire season.

Here is the breadth of Christmas celebration in carols (with translations from the French and German), ballads, children's rhyme, and biblical verse complete with Mary, Joseph, and the baby Jesus in the manger. In this collection great poets such as Milton, Donne, Smart, Coleridge, Tennyson, Wordsworth, Hardy, Eliot, Frost, Rossetti, Teasdale, Browning, Dunbar, Hughes, Stevenson, and Carroll honor Noël.

See the familiar holiday trimmings here: the winter wonderland of snow, the Christmas tree, holly trimmed with bay, and the strategically placed mistletoe. Enjoy the traditional foods: goose, mince pie, pudding, sugar plums, and the welcome cup of wassail. Be reminded of the need for charity to others less fortunate. Reexperience how as a child—naughty or nice—you tried to snow your parents with feigned good behavior or vented disappointment over the unwanted or utilitarian gift and how as adults you enjoy renewed youth in assembling and playing with toys that light up children's eyes.

The merry associations of the season come alive in *Christmas Poems*—a gift for both yourself and those you love. Share joyous memories and forge new ones as you sing these carols and read these poems.

—DAVID STANFORD BURR

CHRISTMAS POEMS

❧ Angels We Have Heard on High

Angels we have heard on high,
Sweetly singing o'er the plain,
And the mountains in reply,
Echoing their joyous strain.

Gloria in excelsis Deo,
Gloria in excelsis Deo!

Shepherds, why this jubilee?
Why your joyful strains prolong?
What the gladsome tidings be
Which inspire your heav'nly song?

Gloria in excelsis Deo,
Gloria in excelsis Deo!

Come to Bethlehem and see
Him whose birth the angels sing;
Come adore on bended knee
Christ, the Lord, the new-born King.

Gloria in excelsis Deo,
Gloria in excelsis Deo!

continues

TRADITIONAL CAROL

See Him in a manger laid,
Whom the choir of angels praise;
Holy Spirit, lend thine aid,
While our hearts in love we raise.

Gloria in excelsis Deo,
Gloria in excelsis Deo!

TRADITIONAL CAROL

❧ As Joseph Was A-Walking

As Joseph was a-walking
  He heard Angels sing,
"This night shall be born
  Our Heavenly King.

"He neither shall be born
  In house nor in hall,
Nor in the place of paradise,
  But in an ox-stall.

"He shall not be clothèd
  In purple nor pall;
But all in fair linen,
  As wear babies all.

"He shall not be rockèd
  In silver nor gold,
But in a wooden cradle
  That rocks on the mould.

"He neither shall be christened
  In milk nor in wine,
But in pure spring-well water
  Fresh spring from Bethine."

continues

ANONYMOUS

Mary took her baby,
  She dressed Him so sweet,
She laid Him in a manger,
  All there for to sleep.

As she stood over Him
  She heard Angels sing,
"Oh, bless our dear Saviour
  Our Heavenly King!"

ANONYMOUS

❧ Away in a Manger

Away in a manger, no crib for a bed,
The little Lord Jesus laid down his sweet head.
The stars in the sky looked down where he lay,
The little Lord Jesus asleep in the hay.

The cattle are lowing, the baby awakes,
But little Lord Jesus no crying he makes.
I love Thee, Lord Jesus, look down from the sky
And stay by my side 'til morning is nigh.

Be near me, Lord Jesus, I ask Thee to stay
Close by me forever, and love me, I pray.
Bless all the dear children in thy tender care,
And fit us for heaven, to live with Thee there.

❧ Bells Across the Snows

O Christmas, merry Christmas!
   Is it really come again,
With its memories and greetings,
   With its joy and with its pain?
There's a minor in the carol,
   And a shadow in the light,
And a spray of cypress twining
   With the holly wreath to-night.
And the hush is never broken
   By laughter light and low,
As we listen in the starlight
   To the "bells across the snow."

O Christmas, merry Christmas!
   'Tis not so very long
Since other voices blended
   With the carol and the song!
If we could but hear them singing
   As they are singing now,
If we could but see the radiance
   Of the crown on each dear brow;
There would be no sigh to smother,
   No hidden tear to flow,
As we listen in the starlight
   To the "bells across the snow."

O Christmas, merry Christmas!
  This never more can be;
We cannot bring again the days
  Of our unshadowed glee.
But Christmas, happy Christmas,
  Sweet herald of good-will,
With holy songs of glory
  Brings holy gladness still.
For peace and hope may brighten,
  And patient love may glow,
As we listen in the starlight
  To the "bells across the snow."

Bethlehem of Judea

A little child,
A shining star.
A stable rude,
The door ajar.

Yet in that place,
So crude, forlorn,
The Hope of all
The world was born.

ANONYMOUS

❧ The Boy Who Laughed at Santa Claus

In Baltimore there lived a boy.
He wasn't anybody's joy.
Although his name was Jabez Dawes,
His character was full of flaws.
In school he never led the classes,
He hid old ladies' reading glasses,
His mouth was open while he chewed,
And elbows to the table glued.
He stole the milk of hungry kittens,
And walked through doors marked No Admittance.
He said he acted thus because
There wasn't any Santa Claus.
Another trick that tickled Jabez
Was crying "Boo!" at little babies.
He brushed his teeth, they said in town,
Sideways instead of up and down.
Yet people pardoned every sin
And viewed his antics with a grin
Till they were told by Jabez Dawes,
"There isn't any Santa Claus!"
Deploring how he did behave,
His parents quickly sought their grave.

continues

OGDEN NASH (1902–1971)   9

They hurried through the portals pearly,
And Jabez left the funeral early.
Like whooping cough, from child to child,
He sped to spread the rumor wild:
"Sure as my name is Jabez Dawes
There isn't any Santa Claus!"
Slunk like a weasel or a marten
Through nursery and kindergarten,
Whispering low to every tot,
"There isn't any, no, there's not!
No beard, no pipe, no scarlet clothes,
No twinkling eyes, no cherry nose,
No sleigh, and furthermore, by Jiminy,
Nobody coming down the chimney!"
The children wept all Christmas Eve
And Jabez chortled up his sleeve.
No infant dared to hang up his stocking
For fear of Jabez' ribald mocking.
He sprawled on his untidy bed,
Fresh malice dancing in his head,
When presently with scalp a-tingling,
Jabez heard a distant jingling;
He heard the crunch of sleigh and hoof
Crisply alighting on the roof.
What good to rise and bar the door?
A shower of soot was on the floor.
Jabez beheld, oh, awe of awes,
The fireplace full of Santa Claus!

OGDEN NASH (1902–1971)

Then Jabez fell upon his knees
With cries of "Don't," and "Pretty please."
He howled, "I don't know where you read it.
I swear some other fellow said it!"
"Jabez," replied the angry saint,
"It isn't I, it's you that ain't.
Although there *is* a Santa Claus,
There isn't any Jabez Dawes!"
Said Jabez then with impudent vim,
"Oh, yes there is; and I am him!
Your language don't scare me, it doesn't—"
And suddenly he found he wasn't!
From grinning feet to unkempt locks
Jabez became a jack-in-the-box,
An ugly toy in Santa's sack,
Mounting the flue on Santa's back.
The neighbors heard his mournful squeal;
They searched for him, but not with zeal.
No trace was found of Jabez Dawes,
Which led to thunderous applause,
And people drank a loving cup
And went and hung their stockings up.
All you who sneer at Santa Claus,
Beware the fate of Jabez Dawes,
The saucy boy who told the saint off;
The child who got him, licked his paint off.

❧ Carol

I sing the birth was born to-night,
The author both of life and light;
  The angels so did sound it,
And, like the ravished shepherds said,
Who saw the light, and were afraid,
  Yet searched, and true they found it.

The Son of God, the eternal king,
That did us all salvation bring,
  And freed our soul from danger,
He whom the whole world could not take,
The Word, which heaven and earth did make,
  Was now laid in a manger.

The Father's wisdom willed it so,
The Son's obedience knew no No;
  Both wills were in one stature,
And, as that wisdom had decreed,
The Word was now made flesh indeed,
  And took on him our nature.

What comfort by him we do win,
Who made himself the price of sin,
  To make us heirs of glory!
To see this babe, all innocence,
A martyr born in our defence,
  Can man forget the story?

BEN JONSON (1572–1637)

❦ Carol of the Brown King

Of the three Wise Men
Who came to the King,
One was a brown man,
So they sing.

Of the three Wise Men
Who followed the Star,
One was a brown king
From afar.

They brought fine gifts
Of spices and gold
In jeweled boxes
Of beauty untold.

Unto His humble
Manger they came
And bowed their heads
In Jesus' name.

Three Wise Men,
One dark like me—
Part of His
Nativity.

LANGSTON HUGHES (1902–1967)

❧ Ceremony Upon Candlemas Eve

Down with the rosemary, and so
Down with the bays and mistletoe;
Down with the holly, ivy, all
Wherewith ye dressed the Christmas hall;
That so the superstitious find
No one least branch there left behind;
For look, how many leaves there be
Neglected there, maids, trust to me,
So many goblins you shall see.

ROBERT HERRICK (1591–1674)

❧ A Child This Day Is Born

A child this day is born,
   A child of high renown,
Most worthy of a sceptre,
   A sceptre and a crown:

    Noël, Noël, Noël,
      Noël, sing all we may,
    Because the King of all kings
      Was born this blessed day.

These tidings shepherds heard,
   In field watching their fold,
Were by an angel unto them
   That night revealed and told:

To whom the angel spoke,
   Saying, "Be not afraid;
Be glad, poor silly shepherds —
   Why are you so dismayed?

"For lo! I bring you tidings
   Of gladness and of mirth,
Which cometh to all people by
   This holy infant's birth":

continues

Then was there with the angel
　An host incontinent
Of heavenly bright soldiers,
　Which from the Highest was sent:

Lauding the Lord our God,
　And his celestial King;
All glory be in Paradise,
　This heavenly host did sing:

And as the angel told them,
　So to them did appear;
They found the young child, Jesus Christ,
　With Mary, his mother dear:

　Noël, Noël, Noël,
　　Noël, sing all we may,
　Because the King of all kings
　　Was born this blessed day.

❧ A Child's Christmas Day

He opens his eyes with a cry of delight,
There's a toy-shop all round him, a wonderful sight!
The fairies have certainly called in the night.

They are quiet at first—both the girls and the boys,
Too happy to make any riot or noise,
And they mutually show to each other their toys.

Then Uncle appears with a smile on his lips,
As his fingers deep down in his pocket he dips,
A performance which ends in a series of 'tips'.

Next Sally brings Pudding—the spirit burns blue,
They all dance around her, a merry young crew,
For they hope to eat mince-pie and plum-pudding too.

But, see! In the nursery a terrible racket,
The dolls lose their heads, there are rents in
    each jacket,
And if you've a toy, it's the fashion to crack it.

The floor is all littered with signs of the fray,
He is sulky and tired with much eating and play,
And Nurse too is cross as she bears him away.

❧ Christmas

All after pleasures as I rid one day,
   My horse and I, both tir'd, bodie and minde,
   With full crie of affections, quite astray,
I took up in the next inne I could finde.
There when I came, whom found I but my deare,
   My dearest Lord, expecting till the grief
   Of pleasures brought me to him, readie there
To be all passengers most sweet relief?
O Thou, whose glorious, yet contracted light,
   Wrapt in nights mantle, stole into a manger;
   Since my dark soul and brutish is thy right,
To Man of all beasts be not thou a stranger:
   Furnish & deck my soul, that thou mayst have
   A better lodging then a rack or grave.

The shepherds sing; and shall I silent be?
      My God, no hymne for thee?
My soul's a shepherd too; a flock it feeds
      Of thoughts, and words, and deeds.
The pasture is thy word: the streams, thy grace
      Enriching all the place.
Shepherd and flock shall sing, and all my powers
      Out-sing the day-light houres.

stanza continues

Then we will chide the sunne for letting night
        Take up his place and right:
We sing one common Lord; wherefore he should
        Himself the candle hold.
I will go searching, till I find a sunne
        Shall stay, till we have done;
A willing shiner, that shall shine as gladly,
        As frost-nipt sunnes look sadly.
Then we will sing, and shine all our own day,
        And one another pay:
His beams shall cheer my breast, and both so twine,
Till ev'n his beams sing, and my musick shine.

❧ Christmas at Sea

The sheets were frozen hard, and they cut the
    naked hand;
The decks were like a slide, where a seaman scarce
    could stand;
The wind was a nor'wester, blowing squally off
    the sea;
And cliffs and spouting breakers were the only
    things a-lee.

They heard the surf a-roaring before the break
    of day;
But 'twas only with the peep of light we saw how
    ill we lay.
We tumbled every hand on deck instanter, with
    a shout,
And we gave her the maintops'l, and stood by to
    go about.

All day we tacked and tacked between the South
    Head and the North;
All day we hauled the frozen sheets, and got no
    further forth;
All day as cold as charity, in bitter pain and dread,
For very life and nature we tacked from head to
    head.

We gave the South a wider berth, for there the
　　tide-race roared;
But every tack we made we brought the North
　　Head close aboard;
So's we saw the cliffs and houses, and the breakers
　　running high,
And the coastguard in his garden, with his glass
　　against his eye.

The frost was on the village roofs as white as
　　ocean foam;
The good red fires were burning bright in every
　　'longshore home;
The windows sparkled clear, and the chimneys
　　volleyed out;
And I vow we sniffed the victuals as the vessel
　　went about.

The bells upon the church were rung with a mighty
　　jovial cheer;
For it's just that I should tell you how (of all days
　　in the year)
This day of our adversity was blessèd Christmas
　　morn,
And the house above the coastguard's was the
　　house where I was born.

continues

O well I saw the pleasant room, the pleasant
    faces there,
My mother's silver spectacles, my father's
    silver hair;
And well I saw the firelight, like a flight of
    homely elves,
Go dancing round the china-plates that stand
    upon the shelves.

And well I knew the talk they had, the talk that
    was of me,
Of the shadow on the household and the son that
    went to sea;
And O the wicked fool I seemed, in every kind
    of way,
To be here and hauling frozen ropes on blessèd
    Christmas Day.

They lit the high sea-light, and the dark began
    to fall.
"All hands to loose topgallant sails," I heard the
    captain call.
"By the Lord, she'll never stand it," our first mate,
    Jackson, cried.
. . . "It's the one way or the other, Mr. Jackson,"
    he replied.

She staggered to her bearings, but the sails were
    new and good,
And the ship smelt up to windward just as though
    she understood.
As the winter's day was ending, in the entry of
    the night,
We cleared the weary headland, and passed below
    the light.

And they heaved a mighty breath, every soul on
    board but me,
As they saw her nose again pointing handsome out
    to sea;
But all that I could think of, in the darkness and
    the cold,
Was just that I was leaving home and my folks
    were growing old.

❧ Christmas Bells

I heard the bells on Christmas Day
Their old, familiar carols play,
    And wild and sweet
    The words repeat
Of peace on earth, good-will to men!

And thought how, as the day had come,
The belfries of all Christendom
    Had rolled along
    The unbroken song
Of peace on earth, good-will to men!

Till, ringing, swinging on its way,
The world revolved from night to day
    A voice, a chime,
    A chant sublime
Of peace on earth, good-will to men!

Then from each black, accursèd mouth
The cannon thundered in the South
    And with the sound
    The carols drowned
Of peace on earth, good-will to men!

It was as if an earthquake rent
The hearth-stones of a continent,
  And made forlorn
  The households born
Of peace on earth, good-will to men!

And in despair I bowed my head;
"There is no peace on earth," I said;
  "For hate is strong
  And mocks the song
Of peace on earth, good-will to men!"

Then pealed the bells more loud and deep,
"God is not dead; nor doth He sleep!
  The Wrong shall fail,
  The Right prevail,
With peace on earth, good-will to men!"

❦ A Christmas Carmen

Sound over all waters, reach out from all lands,
The chorus of voices, the clasping of hands;
Sing hymns that were sung by the stars of the morn,
Sing songs of the angels when Jesus was born!
>   With glad jubilations
>   Bring hope to the nations!
The dark night is ending and dawn has begun:
Rise, hope of the ages, arise like the sun,
>   All speech flow to music, all hearts beat as one!

Sing the bridal of nations! with chorals of love
Sing out the war-vulture and sing in the dove,
Till the hearts of the peoples keep time in accord,
And the voice of the world is the voice of the Lord!
>   Clasp hands of the nations
>   In strong gratulations:
The dark night is ending and dawn has begun;
Rise, hope of the ages, arise like the sun,
>   All speech flow to music, all hearts beat as one.

Blow, bugles of battle, the marches of peace;
East, west, north, and south let the long quarrel cease:
Sing the song of great joy that the angels began,
Sing of glory to God and of good-will to man!

stanza continues

JOHN GREENLEAF WHITTIER (1807–1892)

Hark! joining in chorus
The heavens bend o'er us!
The dark night is ending and dawn has begun;
Rise, hope of the ages, arise like the sun,
All speech flow to music, all hearts beat as one!

❧ A Christmas Carol

The Christ-child lay on Mary's lap,
  His hair was like a light.
(O weary, weary were the world,
  But here is all aright.)

The Christ-child lay on Mary's breast,
  His hair was like a star.
(O stern and cunning are the kings,
  But here the true hearts are.)

The Christ-child lay on Mary's heart,
  His hair was like a fire.
(O weary, weary is the world,
  But here the world's desire.)

The Christ-child stood at Mary's knee,
  His hair was like a crown,
And all the flowers looked up at Him,
  And all the stars looked down.

G. K. CHESTERTON (1874–1936)

🌜 A Christmas Carol

The shepherds went their hasty way,
   And found the lowly stable-shed
Where the virgin-mother lay:
   And now they checked their eager tread,
For to the babe, that at her bosom clung,
A mother's song the virgin-mother sung.

They told her how a glorious light,
   Streaming from a heavenly throng,
Around them shone, suspending night;
   While sweeter than a mother's song,
Blessed angels heralded the Saviour's birth,
Glory to God on high! and peace on earth.

She listened to the tale divine,
   And closer still the babe she pressed;
And while she cried, "The babe is mine!"
   The milk rushed faster to her breast:
Joy rose within her, like a summer's morn:
Peace, peace on earth! the Prince of peace is born.

Thou mother of the Prince of peace,
   Poor, simple, and of low estate;
That strife should vanish, battle cease,
   Oh! why should this thy soul elate?

stanza continues

SAMUEL TAYLOR COLERIDGE (1772–1834)   29

Sweet music's loudest note, the poet's story,
Didst thou ne'er love to hear of fame and glory?

And is not War a youthful king,
   A stately hero clad in mail?
Beneath his footsteps laurels spring;
   Him earth's majestic monarchs hail!
Their friend, their playmate! and his bold bright eye
Compels the maiden's love-confessing sigh.

"Tell this in some more courtly scene,
   To maids and youths in robes of state!
I am a woman poor and mean,
   And therefore is my soul elate.
War is a ruffian, all with guilt defiled,
That from the aged father tears his child!

"A murderous fiend, by fiends adored,
   He kills the sire and starves the son,
The husband kills, and from her board
   Steals all his widow's toil had won;
Plunders God's world of beauty; rends away
All safety from the night, all comfort from the day.

"Then wisely is my soul elate,
   That strife should vanish, battle cease;

stanza continues

I'm poor, and of a low estate,
    The mother of the Prince of peace!
Joy rises in me, like a summer's morn;
Peace, peace on earth! the Prince of peace is born!"

❧ A Christmas Carol

So now is come our joyful feast,
   Let every man be jolly;
Each room with ivy leaves is dressed,
   And every post with holly.
     Though some churls at our mirth repine,
     Round your foreheads garlands twine,
     Drown sorrow in a cup of wine,
   And let us all be merry.

Now all our neighbors' chimnies smoke,
   And Christmas blocks are burning;
Their ovens they with baked meats choke,
   And all their spits are turning.
     Without the door let sorrow lie,
     And if for cold it hap to die,
     We'll bury it in a Christmas pie,
   And evermore be merry.

Now every lad is wondrous trim,
   And no man minds his labor;
Our lasses have provided them
   A bagpipe and a tabor.
     Young men and maids, and girls and boys,
     Give life to one another's joys;
     And you anon shall by their noise
   Perceive that they are merry.

GEORGE WITHER (1588–1667)

Rank misers now do sparing shun,
　　Their hall of music soundeth;
And dogs thence with whole shoulders run,
　　So all things aboundeth.
　　　　The country-folk themselves advance,
　　　　For crowdy-mutton's come out of France;
　　　　And Jack shall pipe and Jill shall dance,
　　　　And all the town be merry.

Ned Swatch hath fetched his bands from pawn,
　　And all his best apparel;
Brisk Nell hath bought a ruff of lawn
　　With droppings of the barrel.
　　　　And those that hardly all the year
　　　　Had bread to eat or rags to wear,
　　　　Will have both clothes and dainty fare,
　　　　And all the day be merry.

Now poor men to the justices
　　With capons make their errands;
And if they hap to fail of these,
　　They plague them with their warrants.
　　　　But now they feed them with good cheer,
　　　　And what they want they take in beer,
　　　　For Christmas comes but once a year,
　　　　And then they shall be merry.

continues

GEORGE WITHER (1588–1667)　　　　　　　33

Good farmers in the country nurse
  The poor, that else were undone;
Some landlords spend their money worse,
  On lust and pride at London.
    There the roisters they do play,
    Drab and dice their land away,
    Which may be ours another day;
  And therefore let's be merry.

The client now his suit forbears,
  The prisoner's heart is eased;
The debtor drinks away his cares,
  And for the time is pleased.
    Though others' purses be more fat,
    Why should we pine or grieve at that;
    Hang sorrow, care will kill a cat,
  And therefore let's be merry.

Hark how the wags abroad do call
  Each other forth to rambling;
Anon you'll see them in the hall,
  For nuts and apples scrambling;
    Hark how the roofs with laughters sound,
    Anon they'll think the house goes round;
    For they the cellar's depths have found,
  And there they will be merry.

The wenches with their wassail-bowls
   About the streets are singing;
The boys are come to catch the owls,
   The wild mare in is bringing.
     Our kitchen boy hath broke his box,
     And to the dealing of the ox
     Our honest neighbors come by flocks,
   And here they will be merry.

Now kings and queens poor sheep-cotes have,
   And mate with everybody;
The honest now may play the knave,
   And wise men play at noddy.
     Some youths will now a mumming go,
     Some others play at rowland-hoe,
     And twenty other gameboys moe;
   Because they will be merry.

Then wherefore in these merry days
   Should we, I pray, be duller?
No, let us sing some roundelays
   To make our mirth the fuller.
     And whilst we thus inspired sing,
     Let all the streets with echoes ring;
     Woods, and hills, and everything
   Bear witness we are merry.

❧ Christmas Carol

Ring out, ye bells!
All Nature swells
With gladness of the wondrous story,
The world was lorn,
But Christ is born
To change our sadness into glory.

Sing, earthlings, sing!
To-night a King
Hath come from heaven's high throne to bless us.
The outstretched hand
O'er all the land
Is raised in pity to caress us.

Come at His call;
Be joyful all;
Away with mourning and with sadness!
The heavenly choir
With holy fire
Their voices raise in songs of gladness.

The darkness breaks
And Dawn awakes,

stanza continues

Her cheeks suffused with youthful blushes.
The rocks and stones
In holy tones
Are singing sweeter than the thrushes.

Then why should we
In silence be,
When Nature lends her voice to praises;
When heaven and earth
Proclaim the truth
Of Him for whom that lone star blazes?

No, be not still,
But with a will
Strike all your harps and set them ringing;
On hill and heath
Let every breath
Throw all its power into singing!

❧ Christmas Carol

Villagers all, this frosty tide,
Let your doors swing open wide,
Though wind may follow and snow betide
Yet draw us in by your fire to bide:
  Joy shall be yours in the morning.

Here we stand in the cold and the sleet,
Blowing fingers and stamping feet,
Come from far away, you to greet —
You by the fire and we in the street —
  Bidding you joy in the morning.

For ere one half of the night was gone,
Sudden a star has led us on,
Raining bliss and benison —
Bliss tomorrow and more anon,
  Joy for every morning.

Good man Joseph toiled through the snow —
Saw the star o'er the stable low;
Mary she might not farther go —
Welcome thatch and litter below!
  Joy was hers in the morning.

KENNETH GRAHAME (1859–1932)

And then they heard the angels tell,
"Who were the first to cry noël?
Animals all as it befell,
In the stable where they did dwell!
    Joy shall be theirs in the morning."

❧ Christmas Carol

The kings they came from out the south,
   All dressed in ermine fine;
They bore Him gold and chrysoprase,
   And gifts of precious wine.

The shepherds came from out the north,
   Their coats were brown and old;
They brought Him little new-born lambs—
   They had not any gold.

The wise men came from out the east,
   And they were wrapped in white;
The star that led them all the way
   Did glorify the night.

The angels came from heaven high,
   And they were clad with wings;
And lo, they brought a joyful song
   The host of heaven sings.

The kings they knocked upon the door,
   The wise men entered in,
The shepherds followed after them
   To hear the song begin.

SARA TEASDALE (1884–1933)

The angels sang through all the night
    Until the rising sun,
But little Jesus fell asleep
    Before the song was done.

❧ The Christmas Carol

The minstrels played their Christmas tune
   To-night beneath my cottage eaves;
While, smitten by a lofty moon,
   The encircling laurels, thick with leaves,
Gave back a rich and dazzling sheen
That overpowered their natural green.

Through hill and valley every breeze
   Had sunk to rest, with folded wings:
Keen was the air, but could not freeze
   Nor check the music of the strings;
So stout and hardy were the band
That scraped the chords with strenuous hand!

And who but listened—till was paid
   Respect to every inmate's claim:
The greeting given, the music played,
   In honor of each household name,
Duly pronounced with lusty call,
And "Merry Christmas" wished to all!

How touching, when, at midnight, sweep
   Snow-muffled winds, and all is dark,

stanza continues

WILLIAM WORDSWORTH (1770–1850)

To hear, and sink again to sleep!
   Or, at an earlier call, to mark
By blazing fire, the still suspense
Of self-complacent innocence;

The mutual nod,—the grave disguise
   Of hearts with gladness brimming o'er;
And some unbidden tears that rise
   For names once heard, and heard no more;
Tears brightened by the serenade
For infant in the cradle laid.

Hail ancient Manners! sure defence,
   Where they survive, of wholesome laws;
Remnants of love whose modest sense
   Thus into narrow room withdraws;
Hail, Usages of pristine mould,
And ye that guard them, Mountains old!

❧ Christmas Day

I wonder on that Christmas night
    How many passers-by
Beheld that strange and lustrous light
    In Bethlehem's patch of sky?
We know how the shepherds chanced to be
    Unto the stable sent,
But did that star some rich man see
    And wonder what it meant?

They've told us of the crowded inn
    And of the laughter gay;
But was there none who entered in
    On that first Christmas Day
To say he'd seen a wondrous sight
    And bear the news to them
That God had hung a beacon light
    High over Bethlehem?

Of all the throng that hurried by
    Did no one lift his eyes
To read the glory of the sky?
    Were all so worldly-wise
That God should bid the angels sing,
    Upon that midnight clear,
An anthem to the new-born King
    And only shepherds hear?

EDGAR GUEST (1881–1959)

I wonder is it still the same?
  Are we beyond His reach?
Have we, pursuing wealth and fame,
  Grown deaf to gentler speech?
Should such a strange thing come to be
  And angel choirs appear,
Would only watchful shepherds see
  And thoughtful shepherds hear?

❧ Christmas Eve

Christmas hath a darkness
  Brighter than the blazing noon,
Christmas hath a chillness
  Warmer than the heat of June,
Christmas hath a beauty
  Lovelier than the world can show:
For Christmas bringeth Jesus,
  Brought for us so low.

Earth, strike up your music,
  Birds that sing and bells that ring;
Heaven hath answering music
  For all Angels soon to sing:
Earth, put on your whitest
  Bridal robe of spotless snow:
For Christmas bringeth Jesus,
Brought for us so low.

❧ Christmas Everywhere

Everywhere, everywhere, Christmas tonight!
Christmas in lands of the fir-tree and pine,
Christmas in lands of the palm-tree and vine,
Christmas where snow peaks stand solemn and white,
Christmas where cornfields stand sunny and bright.
Christmas where children are hopeful and gay,
Christmas where old men are patient and gray,
Christmas where peace, like a dove in his flight,
Broods o'er brave men in the thick of the fight;
Everywhere, everywhere, Christmas tonight!
For the Christ-child who comes is the Master of all;
No palace too great, no cottage too small.

PHILLIPS BROOKS (1835–1893)

❧ A Christmas Ghost-Story

(Christmas-eve 1899)

South of the Line, inland from far Durban,
A mouldering soldier lies—your countryman.
Awry and doubled up are his gray bones,
And on the breeze his puzzled phantom moans
Nightly to clear Canopus: "I would know
By whom and when the All-Earth-gladdening Law
Of Peace, brought in by that Man Crucified,
Was ruled to be inept, and set aside?
And what of logic or of truth appears
In tacking 'Anno Domini' to the years?
Near twenty-hundred liveried thus have hied,
But tarries yet the Cause for which He died."

❧ Christmas Greeting from a Fairy to a Child

Lady, dear, if Fairies may
  For a moment lay aside
Cunning tricks and elfish play,
  'Tis at happy Christmas-tide.

We have heard the children say—
  Gentle children, whom we love—
Long ago on Christmas Day,
  Came a message from above.

Still, as Christmas-tide comes round,
  They remember it again—
Echo still the joyful sound
  "Peace on earth, good-will to men!"

Yet the hearts must childlike be
  Where such heavenly guests abide;
Unto children, in their glee,
  All the year is Christmas-tide!

Thus, forgetting tricks and play
  For a moment, Lady dear,
We would wish you, if we may,
  Merry Christmas, glad New Year!

LEWIS CARROLL (1832–1898)   49

❧ The Christmas Holly

The holly! the holly! oh, twine it with bay—
    Come give the holly a song;
For it helps to drive stern winter away,
    With his garment so sombre and long;

It peeps through the trees with its berries of red,
    And its leaves of burnished green,
When the flowers and fruits have long been dead,
    And not even the daisy is seen.
Then sing to the holly, the Christmas holly,
    That hangs over peasant and king;
While we laugh and carouse 'neath its glittering
        boughs,
    To the Christmas holly we'll sing.

The gale may whistle, the frost may come
    To fetter the gurgling rill;
The woods may be bare, and warblers dumb,
    But holly is beautiful still.
In the revel and light of princely halls
    The bright holly branch is found;
And its shadow falls on the lowliest walls,
    While the brimming horn goes round.

ELIZA COOK (1818–1889)

The ivy lives long, but its home must be
  Where graves and ruins are spread;
There's beauty about the cypress tree,
  But it flourishes near the dead;
The laurel the warrior's brow may wreathe,
  But it tells of tears and blood;
I sing the holly, and who can breathe
  Aught of that that is not good?
Then sing to the holly, the Christmas holly,
  That hangs over peasant and king;
While we laugh and carouse 'neath its glittering
    boughs,
  To the Christmas holly we'll sing.

❧ Christmas Is Coming

Christmas is coming,
   The Goose is getting fat,
Please put a penny in the old man's hat.
    If you haven't a penny, a ha' penny will do,
    If you haven't a ha' penny—God bless you!

❧ A Christmas Letter from Australia

'Tis Christmas, and the North wind blows; 'twas
    two years yesterday
Since from the Lusitania's bows I looked o'er
    Table Bay,
A tripper round the narrow world, a pilgrim of
    the main,
Expecting when her sails unfurled to start for
    home again.

'Tis Christmas, and the North wind blows; today
    our hearts are one,
Though you are 'mid the English snows and I in
    Austral sun;
You, when you hear the Northern blast, pile high a
    mightier fire,
Our ladies cower until it's past in lawn and lace attire.

I fancy I can picture you upon this Christmas
    night,
Just sitting as you used to do, the laughter at
    its height;
And then a sudden, silent pause intruding on
    your glee,
And kind eyes glistening because you chanced to
    think of me.

continues

DOUGLAS SLADEN (1856–1947)   53

This morning when I woke and knew 'twas
    Christmas come again,
I almost fancied I could view white rime upon
    the pane,
And hear the ringing of the wheels upon the frosty
    ground,
And see the drip that downward steals in icy casket
    bound.

I daresay you'll be on the lake, or sliding on
    the snow,
And breathing on your hands to make the
    circulation flow,
Nestling your nose among the furs of which your
    boa's made, —
The Fahrenheit here registers a hundred in the
    shade.

It is not quite a Christmas here with this un-
    clouded sky,
This pure transparent atmosphere, this sun mid-
    heaven-high;
To see the rose upon the bush, young leaves upon
    the trees,
And hear the forest's summer hush or the low hum
    of bees.

But cold winds bring not Christmastide, nor
  budding roses June,
And when it's night upon your side we're basking
  in the noon.
Kind hearts make Christmas—June can bring blue
  sky or clouds above;
The only universal spring is that which comes
  of love.

And so it's Christmas in the South as on the North-
  sea coasts,
Though we are staved with summer-drouth and
  you with winter frosts.
And we shall have our roast beef here, and think of
  you the while,
Though all the watery hemisphere cuts off the
  mother isle.

Feel sure that we shall think of you, we who have
  wandered forth,
And many a million thoughts will go to-day from
  south to north;
Old heads will muse on churches old, where bells
  will ring to-day—
The very bells, perchance, which tolled their
  fathers to the clay.

continues

DOUGLAS SLADEN (1856–1947)

And now, good-night! and I shall dream that I am
    with you all,
Watching the ruddy embers gleam athwart the
    panelled hall;
Nor care I if I dream or not, though severed by
    the foam,
My heart is always in the spot which was my
    childhood's home.

❧ Christmas Morning

If Bethlehem were here today
   Or this were very long ago,
There wouldn't be a winter time
   Nor any cold or snow.

I'd run out through the garden gate,
   And down along the pasture walk;
And off beside the cattle barns
   I'd hear a kind of gentle talk.

I'd move the heavy iron chain
   And pull away the wooden pin;
I'd push the door a little bit
   And tiptoe very softly in.

The pigeons and the yellow hens
   And all the cows would stand away;
Their eyes would open wide to see
   A lady in the manger hay,
If this were very long ago
   And Bethlehem were here today.

And Mother held my hand and smiled—
   I mean the lady would—and she

stanza continues

ELIZABETH MADOX ROBERTS (1881–1941)   57

Would take the woolly blankets off
    Her little boy so I could see.

His shut-up eyes would be asleep,
    And he would look just like our John,
And he would be all crumpled too,
    And have a pinkish color on.

I'd watch his breath go in and out,
    His little clothes would be all white,
I'd slip my finger in his hand
    To feel how he could hold it tight.

And she would smile and say, "Take care,"
    The Mother, Mary, would, "Take care";
And I would kiss his little hand
    And touch his hair.

While Mary put the blankets back
    The gentle talk would soon begin,
And when I'd tiptoe softly out
    I'd meet the wise men going in.

❧ The Christmas Pudding

Into the basin put the plums,
Stirabout, stirabout, stirabout!

Next the good white flour comes,
Stirabout, stirabout, stirabout!

Sugar and peel and eggs and spice.
Stirabout, stirabout, stirabout!

Mix them and fix them and cook them twice.
Stirabout, stirabout, stirabout.

❧ The Christmas Silence

Hushed are the pigeons cooing low,
   On dusty rafters of the loft;
   And mild-eyed oxen, breathing soft,
Sleep on the fragrant hay below.

Dim shadows in the corners hide;
   The glimmering lantern's rays are shed,
   Where one young lamb just lifts his head
Then huddles against his mother's side.

Strange silence tingles in the air;
   Through the half-open door a bar
   Of light from one low hanging star
Touches a baby's radiant hair—

No sound—The mother, kneeling, lays
   Her cheek against the little face.
   Oh, human love! Oh, heavenly grace!
Tis yet in silence that she prays!

Ages of silence end to-night;
   Then to the long expectant earth
   Glad angels come to greet His birth
In burst of music, love and light!

MARGARET DELAND (1857–1945)

❦ Christmas Trees

A Christmas Circular Letter

The city had withdrawn into itself
And left at last the country to the country;
When between whirls of snow not come to lie
And whirls of foliage not yet laid, there drove
A stranger to our yard, who looked the city,
Yet did in country fashion in that there
He sat and waited till he drew us out
A-buttoning coats to ask him who he was.
He proved to be the city come again
To look for something it had left behind
And could not do without and keep its Christmas.
He asked if I would sell my Christmas trees;
My woods—the young fir balsams like a place
Where houses all are churches and have spires.
I hadn't thought of them as Christmas trees.
I doubt if I was tempted for a moment
To sell them off their feet to go in cars
And leave the slope behind the house all bare,
Where the sun shines now no warmer than the moon.
I'd hate to have them know it if I was.
Yet more I'd hate to hold my trees except
As others hold theirs or refuse for them,

stanza continues

Beyond the time of profitable growth,
The trail by market everything must come to.
I dallied so much with the thought of selling.
Then whether from mistaken courtesy
And fear of seeming short of speech, or whether
From hope of hearing good of what was mine,
I said, 'There aren't enough to be worth while.'

'I could soon tell how many they would cut,
You let me look them over.'

  'You could look.
But don't expect I'm going to let you have them.'
Pasture they spring in, some in clumps too close
That lop each other of boughs, but not a few
Quite solitary and having equal boughs
All round and round. The latter he nodded 'Yes' to,
Or paused to say beneath some lovelier one,
With a buyer's moderation, 'That would do.'
I thought so too, but wasn't there to say so.
We climbed the pasture on the south, crossed over,
And came down on the north.

  He said, 'A thousand.'

'A thousand Christmas trees! — at what apiece?'

He felt some need of softening that to me:
'A thousand trees would come to thirty dollars.'
Then I was certain I had never meant
To let him have them. Never show surprise!
But thirty dollars seemed so small beside
The extent of pasture I should strip, three cents
(For that was all they figured out apiece),
Three cents so small beside the dollar friends
I should be writing to within the hour
Would pay in cities for good trees like those,
Regular vestry-trees whole Sunday Schools
Could hang enough on to pick off enough.
A thousand Christmas trees I didn't know I had!
Worth three cents more to give away than sell,
As may be shown by a simple calculation.
Too bad I couldn't lay one in a letter.
I can't help wishing I could send you one,
In wishing you herewith a Merry Christmas.

❧ A Cradle Song

Sweet dreams, form a shade
O'er my lovely infant's head;
Sweet dreams of pleasant streams
By happy, silent, moony beams.

Sweet sleep, with soft down
Weave thy brows an infant crown.
Sweet sleep, Angel mild,
Hover o'er my happy child.

Sweet smiles, in the night
Hover over my delight;
Sweet smiles, mother's smiles,
All the livelong night beguiles.

Sweet moans, dovelike sighs,
Chase not slumber from thy eyes.
Sweet moans, sweeter smiles,
All the dovelike moans beguiles.

Sleep, sleep, happy child,
All creation slept and smil'd;
Sleep, sleep, happy sleep,
While o'er thee thy mother weep.

Sweet babe, in thy face
Holy image I can trace.
Sweet babe once like thee,
Thy Maker lay and wept for me,

Wept for me, for thee, for all,
When He was an infant small.
Thou His image ever see,
Heavenly face that smiles on thee,

Smiles on thee, on me, on all;
Who became an infant small.
Infant smiles are His own smiles;
Heaven and earth to peace beguiles.

❦ December

from *THE SHEPHERD'S CALENDAR*

Christmass is come and every hearth
Makes room to give him welcome now
Een want will dry its tears in mirth
And crown him wi a holly bough
Tho tramping neath a winters sky
Oer snow track paths and rhymey stiles
The huswife sets her spining bye
And bids him welcome wi her smiles
Each house is swept the day before
And windows stuck wi evergreens
The snow is beesomd from the door
And comfort crowns the cottage scenes
Gilt holly wi its thorny pricks
And yew and box wi berrys small
These deck the unusd candlesticks
And pictures hanging by the wall

Neighbours resume their anual cheer
Wishing wi smiles and spirits high
Clad christmass and a happy year
To every morning passer bye
Milk maids their christmass journeys go

stanza continues

JOHN CLARE (1793–1864)

Accompanyd wi favourd swain
And childern pace the crumping snow
To taste their grannys cake again

Hung wi the ivys veining bough
The ash trees round the cottage farm
Are often stript of branches now
The cotters christmass hearth to warm
He swings and twists his hazel band
And lops them off wi sharpend hook
And oft brings ivy in his hand
To decorate the chimney nook

Old winter whipes his ides bye
And warms his fingers till he smiles
Where cottage hearths are blazing high
And labour resteth from his toils
Wi merry mirth beguiling care
Old customs keeping wi the day
Friends meet their christmass cheer to share
And pass it in a harmless way

Old customs O I love the sound
However simple they may be
What ere wi time has sanction found
Is welcome and is dear to me

stanza continues

JOHN CLARE (1793–1864)

Pride grows above simplicity
And spurns it from her haughty mind
And soon the poets song will be
The only refuge they can find

The shepherd now no more afraid
Since custom doth the chance bestow
Starts up to kiss the giggling maid
Beneath the branch of mizzletoe
That neath each cottage beam is seen
Wi pearl-like-berrys shining gay
The shadow still of what hath been
Which fashion yearly fades away

And singers too a merry throng
At early morn wi simple skill
Yet imitate the angels song
And chant their christmass ditty still
And mid the storm that dies and swells
By fits-in humings softly steals
The music of the village bells
Ringing round their merry peals

And when its past a merry crew
Bedeckt in masks and ribbons gay
The 'Morrice danse' their sports renew
And act their winter evening play

stanza continues

JOHN CLARE (1793–1864)

The clown-turnd-kings for penny praise
Storm wi the actors strut and swell
And harlequin a laugh to raise
Wears his hump back and tinkling bell

And oft for pence and spicy ale
Wi winter nosgays pind before
The wassail singer tells her tale
And drawls her christmass carrols oer
The prentice boy wi ruddy face
And ryhme bepowderd dancing locks
From door to door wi happy pace
Runs round to claim his 'christmass box'

The block behind the fire is put
To sanction customs old desires
And many a faggots bands are cut
For the old farmers christmass fires
Where loud tongd gladness joins the throng
And winter meets the warmth of may
Feeling by times the heat too strong
And rubs his shins and draws away

While snows the window panes bedim
The fire curls up a sunny charm
Where creaming oer the pitchers rim
The flowering ale is set to warm

stanza continues

Mirth full of joy as summer bees
Sits there its pleasures to impart
While childern tween their parents knees
Sing scraps of carrols oer by heart

And some to view the winter weathers
Climb up the window seat wi glee
Likening the snow to falling feathers
In fancys infant extacy
Laughing wi superstitious love
Oer visions wild that youth supplyes
Of people pulling geese above
And keeping christmass in the skyes

As tho the homstead trees were drest
In lieu of snow wi dancing leaves
As tho the sundryd martins nest
Instead of ides hung the eaves
The childern hail the happy day
As if the snow was april grass
And pleasd as neath the warmth of may
Sport oer the water froze to glass

Thou day of happy sound and mirth
That long wi childish memory stays
How blest around the cottage hearth
I met thee in my boyish days

stanza continues

Harping wi raptures dreaming joys
On presents that thy coming found
The welcome sight of little toys
The christmass gifts of comers round

The wooden horse wi arching head
Drawn upon wheels around the room
The gilded coach of ginger bread
And many colord sugar plumb
Gilt coverd books for pictures sought
Or storys childhood loves to tell
Wi many a urgent promise bought
To get tomorrows lesson well

And many a thing a minutes sport
Left broken on the sanded floor
When we woud leave our play and court
Our parents promises for more
Tho manhood bids such raptures dye
And throws such toys away as vain
Yet memory loves to turn her eye
And talk such pleasures oer again

Around the glowing hearth at night
The harmless laugh and winter tale
Goes round—while parting friends delight
To toast each other oer their ale

stanza continues

The cotter oft wi quiet zeal
Will musing oer his bible lean
While in the dark the lovers steal
To kiss and toy behind the screen

The yule cake dotted thick wi plumbs
Is on each supper table found
And cats look up for falling crumbs
Which greedy childern litter round
And huswifes sage stuffd seasond chine
Long hung in chimney nook to drye
And boiling eldern berry wine
To drink the christmass eves 'good bye'

❧ Deck the Halls

Deck the halls with boughs of holly.
Fa la la la la, la la la la.
'Tis the season to be jolly.
Fa la la la la, la la la la.
Don we now our gay apparel.
Fa la la, la la la, la la la.
Troll the ancient Yuletide carol:
Fa la la la la, la la la la.

See the blazing Yule before us.
Fa la la la la, la la la la.
Strike the harp and join the chorus.
Fa la la la la, la la la la.
Follow me in merry measure —
Fa la la, la la la, la la la —
While I tell of Yuletide treasure.
Fa la la la la, la la la la.

Fast away the old year passes.
Fa la la la la, la la la la.
Hail the new, ye lads and lasses.
Fa la la la la, la la la la.

stanza continues

TRADITIONAL CAROL

Sing we joyous, all together —
Fa la la, la la la, la la la —
Heedless of the wind and weather.
Fa la la la la, la la la la.

TRADITIONAL CAROL

❧ Eddi's Service

Eddi, priest of St Wilfrid
  In the chapel at Manhood End,
Ordered a midnight service
  For such as cared to attend.

But the Saxons were keeping Christmas,
  And the night was stormy as well.
Nobody came to service,
  Though Eddi rang the bell.

'Wicked weather for walking,'
  Said Eddi of Manhood End.
'But I must go on with the service
  For such as care to attend.'

The altar-lamps were lighted, —
  An old marsh-donkey came,
Bold as a guest invited,
  And stared at the guttering flame.

The storm beat on at the windows,
  The water splashed on the floor,

stanza continues

And a wet, yoke-weary bullock
    Pushed in through the open door.

'How do I know what is greatest,
    How do I know what is least?
That is my Father's business,'
    Said Eddi, Wilfrid's priest.

'But—three are gathered together—
    Listen to me and attend.
I bring good news, my brethren!'
    Said Eddi, of Manhood End.

And he told the Ox of a manger,
    And a stall in Bethlehem,
And he spoke to the Ass of a Rider
    That rode to Jerusalem.

They steamed and dripped in the chancel,
    They listened and never stirred,
While, just as though they were Bishops,
    Eddi preached them The Word.

Till the gale blew off on the marshes
    And the windows showed the day,
And the Ox and the Ass together
    Wheeled and clattered away.

And when the Saxons mocked him,
  Said Eddi of Manhood End,
'I dare not shut His chapel
  On such as care to attend.'

❧ The End of the Play

The play is done—the curtain drops,
   Slow-falling to the prompter's bell:
A moment yet the actor stops,
   And looks around, to say farewell.
It is an irksome word and task;
   And, when he's laughed and said his say,
He shows, as he removes his mask,
   A face that's anything but gay.

One word, ere yet the evening ends,
   Let's close it with a parting rhyme;
And pledge a hand to all young friends,
   As fits the merry Christmas time.
On life's wide scene you, too, have parts
   That fate erelong shall bid you play;
Good-night!—with honest, gentle hearts
   A kindly greeting go alway!

Good-night!—I'd say the griefs, the joys,
   Just hinted in this mimic page,
The triumphs and defeats of boys,
   Are but repeated in our age.
I'd say your woes were not less keen,
   Your hopes more vain than those of men,
Your pangs or pleasures of fifteen
   At forty-five played o'er again.

I'd say we suffer and we strive,
    Not less nor more as men than boys,
With grizzled beards at forty-five
    As erst at twelve in corduroys;
And if, in time of sacred youth,
    We learned at home to love and pray,
Pray Heaven that early love and truth
    May never wholly pass away.

And in the world as in the school
    I'd say how fate may change and shift,
The prize be sometimes to the fool,
    The race not always to the swift:
The strong may yield, the good may fall,
    The great man be a vulgar clown,
The knave be lifted over all,
    The kind cast pitilessly down.

Who knows the inscrutable design?
    Blessèd be He who took and gave!
Why should your mother, Charles, not mine,
    Be weeping at her darling's grave?
We bow to Heaven that willed it so,
    That darkly rules the fate of all,
That sends the respite or the blow,
    That's free to give or to recall.

continues

This crowns his feast with wine and wit, —
   Who brought him to that mirth and state?
His betters, see, below him sit,
   Or hunger hopeless at the gate!
Who bade the mud from Dives's wheel
   To spurn the rags of Lazarus?
Come, brother, in that dust we'll kneel,
   Confessing Heaven that ruled it thus.

So each shall mourn, in life's advance,
   Dear hopes, dear friends, untimely killed;
Shall grieve for many a forfeit chance,
   And longing passion unfulfilled.
Amen! —whatever fate be sent,
   Pray God the heart may kindly glow,
Although the head with cares be bent,
   And whitened with the winter snow!

Come wealth or want, come good or ill,
   Let young and old accept their part,
And bow before the awful will,
   And bear it with an honest heart.
Who misses or who wins the prize,
   Go, lose or conquer, as you can;
But if you fail, or if you rise,
   Be each, pray God, a gentleman!

A gentleman, or old or young!
  (Bear kindly with my humble lays;)
The sacred chorus first was sung
  Upon the first of Christmas days;
The shepherds heard it overhead, —
  The joyful angels raised it then:
"Glory to Heaven on high," it said,
  "And peace on earth to gentle men!"

My song, save this, is little worth;
  I lay the weary pen aside,
And wish you health and love and mirth,
  As fits the solemn Christmas-tide.
As fits the holy Christmas birth,
  Be this, good friends, our carol still:
Be peace on earth, be peace on earth
  To men of gentle will!

❧ The First Noël

The first Noël the angel did say
Was to certain poor shepherds in fields as they lay;
In fields where they lay, keeping their sheep,
In a cold winter's night that was so deep:
Noël, Noël, Noël, Noël,
Born is the King of Israel!

They lookèd up and saw a star,
Shining in the east, beyond them far;
And to the earth it gave great light,
And so it continued both day and night:

And by the light of that same star,
Three Wise Men came from country far;
To seek for a king was their intent,
And to follow the star wheresoever it went:

This star drew nigh to the north-west;
O'er Bethlehem it took its rest,
And there it did both stop and stay
Right over the place where Jesus lay:

Then did they know assuredly
Within that house the King did lie:

stanza continues

ANONYMOUS

One entered in then for to see,
And found the babe in poverty:

Then entered in those Wise Men three,
Fell reverently upon their knee,
And offered there in his présence
Both gold and myrrh and frankincense:

Between an ox-stall and an ass
This child truly there born he was;
For want of clothing they did him lay
All in the manger, among the hay:

Then let us all with one accord
Sing praises to our heavenly Lord,
That hath made heaven and earth of naught,
And with his blood mankind hath bought:

If we in our time shall do well,
We shall be free from death and hell;
For God hath prepared for us all
A resting place in general:
Noël, Noël, Noël, Noël,
Born is the King of Israel!

❧ For the Children or the Grown-Ups?

'Tis the week before Christmas and every night
  As soon as the children are snuggled up tight
And have sleepily murmured their wishes and
    prayers,
  Such fun as goes on in the parlour downstairs!
For Father, Big Brother, and Grandfather too,
  Start in with great vigour their youth to renew.
The grown-ups are having great fun—all is well;
  And they play till it's long past their hour for bed.

They try to solve puzzles and each one enjoys
  The magical thrill of mechanical toys,
Even Mother must play with a doll that can talk,
  And if you assist it, it's able to walk.
It's really no matter if paint may be scratched,
  Or a cogwheel, a nut, or a bolt gets detached;
The grown-ups are having great fun—all is well;
  The children don't know it, and Santa won't tell.

ANONYMOUS

❧ French Noël

Masters, in this Hall,
   Hear ye news to-day
Brought from over sea,
   And ever I you pray.

Noël! Noël! Noël! Noël sing we clear
Holpen are all folk on earth, Born is God's Son so dear:
Noël! Noël! Noël! Noël sing we loud!
God to-day hath poor folk rais'd, And cast down the proud.

Going over the hills,
   Through the milk-white snow,
Heard I ewes bleat
   While the wind did blow.

Shepherds many an one
   Sat among the sheep,
No man spake more word
   Than they had been asleep.

Quoth I "Fellows mine,
   Why this guise sit ye?
Making but dull cheer,
   Shepherds though ye be?

continues

WILLIAM MORRIS (1834–1896)

"Shepherds should of right
  Leap and dance and sing;
Thus to see ye sit
  Is a right strange thing."

Quoth these fellows then,
  "To Bethlem town we go,
To see a mighty Lord
  Lie in a manger low."

"How name ye this Lord,
  Shepherds?" then said I.
"Very *God*," they said,
  "Come from Heaven high."

Then to Bethlem town
  We went two and two
And in a sorry place
  Heard the oxen low.

Therein did we see
  A sweet and goodly May
And a fair old man;
  Upon the straw She lay.

And a little Child
    On Her arm had She;
"Wot ye Who this is?"
    Said the hinds to me.

Ox and ass Him know,
    Kneeling on their knee:
Wondrous joy had I
    This little Babe to see.

This is Christ the Lord
    Masters, be ye glad!
Christmas is come in,
    And no folk should be sad.

Noël! Noël! Noël! Noël sing we clear
Holpen are all folk on earth, Born is God's Son so dear:
Noël! Noël! Noël! Noël sing we loud!
God to-day hath poor folk rais'd, And cast down the proud.

❧ Gates and Doors

A Ballad of Christmas Eve

There was a gentle hostler
   (And blessed be his name!)
He opened up the stable
   The night Our Lady came.
Our Lady and St. Joseph,
   He gave them food and bed,
And Jesus Christ has given him
   A glory round his head.

So let the gate swing open
   However poor the yard,
Lest weary people visit you
   And find their passage barred.
Unlatch the door at midnight
   And let your lantern's glow
Shine out to guide the traveler's feet
   To you across the snow.

There was a courteous hostler
   (He is in Heaven to-night)
He held Our Lady's bridle
   And helped her to alight.

stanza continues

He spread clean straw before her
 Whereon she might lie down,
And Jesus Christ has given him
 An everlasting crown.

Unlock the door this evening
 And let your gate swing wide,
Let all who ask for shelter
 Come speedily inside.
What if your yard be narrow?
 What if your house be small?
There is a Guest is coming
 Will glorify it all.

There was a joyous hostler
 Who knelt on Christmas morn
Beside the radiant manger
 Wherein his Lord was born.
His heart was full of laughter,
 His soul was full of bliss
When Jesus, on His Mother's lap,
 Gave him His hand to kiss.

Unbar your heart this evening
 And keep no stranger out,
Take from your soul's great portal
 The barrier of doubt.

stanza continues

To humble folk and weary
  Give hearty welcoming,
Your breast shall be to-morrow
  The cradle of a King.

JOYCE KILMER (1886–1918)

～ "God bless us every one"

"God bless us every one!" prayed Tiny Tim,
   Crippled, and dwarfed of body, yet so tall
Of soul, we tiptoe earth to look on him,
      High towering over all.

He loved the loveless world, nor dreamed, indeed,
   That it, at best, could give to him, the while,
But pitying glances, when his only need
      Was but a cheery smile.

And thus he prayed, "God bless us every one!"
   Enfolding all the creeds within the span
Of his child-heart; and so, despising none,
      Was nearer saint than man.

I like to fancy God, in Paradise,
   Lifting a finger o'er the rhythmic swing
Of chiming harp and song, with eager eyes
      Turned earthward, listening—

The Anthem stilled—the angels leaning there
   Above the golden walls—the morning sun
Of Christmas bursting flower-like with the prayer,
      "God bless us Every One!"

JAMES WHITCOMB RILEY (1849–1916)

❧ God Rest Ye Merry, Gentlemen

God rest you merry, gentlemen,
Let nothing you dismay,
Remember Christ our Saviour
Was born on Christmas Day,
To save us all from Satan's pow'r,
When we were gone astray.

    O tidings of comfort and joy,
    Comfort and joy,
    O tidings of comfort and joy.

From God our heav'nly Father,
A blessed Angel came,
And unto certain shepherds
Brought tidings of the same;
How that in Bethlehem was born
The son of God by Name.

    O tidings of comfort and joy,
    Comfort and joy,
    O tidings of comfort and joy.

The Shepherds at those tidings
Rejoiced much in mind

stanza continues

And their flocks a-feeding
In tempest, storm, and wind,
And went straightway to Bethlehem
The Son of God to find.

O tidings of comfort and joy,
Comfort and joy,
O tidings of comfort and joy.

And when they came to Bethlehem,
Where our dear Saviour lay,
They found Him in a manger
Where oxen feed on hay;
His mother Mary kneeling down
Unto the Lord did pray.

O tidings of comfort and joy,
Comfort and joy,
O tidings of comfort and joy.

Now to the Lord sing praises,
All you within this place,
And with true love and brotherhood
Each other now embrace;
This holy tide of Christmas
All other doth deface.

continues

O tidings of comfort and joy,
Comfort and joy,
O tidings of comfort and joy.

❧ Good King Wenceslas

Good King Wenceslas looked out,
  On the Feast of Stephen,
When the snow lay round about,
  Deep, and crisp, and even:
Brightly shone the moon that night,
  Though the frost was cruel,
When a poor man came in sight,
  Gathering winter fuel.

'Hither, page, and stand by me,
  If thou know'st it, telling,
Yonder peasant, who is he?
  Where and what his dwelling?'
'Sire, he lives a good league hence,
  Underneath the mountain,
Right against the forest fence,
  By Saint Agnes' fountain.'

'Bring me flesh, and bring me wine,
  Bring me pine-logs hither:
Thou and I will see him dine,
  When we bear them thither.'
Page and monarch, forth they went,
  Forth they went together;

stanza continues

J. M. NEALE (1818–1866)

Through the rude wind's wild lament
    And the bitter weather.

'Sire, the night is darker now,
    And the wind blows stronger;
Fails my heart, I know not how;
    I can go no longer.'
'Mark my footsteps, good my page;
    Tread thou in them boldly:
Thou shalt find the winter's rage
    Freeze thy blood less coldly.'

In his master's steps he trod,
    Where the snow lay dinted;
Heat was in the very sod
    Which the Saint had printed.
Therefore, Christian men, be sure,
    Wealth or rank possessing,
Ye who now will bless the poor,
    Shall yourselves find blessing.

        J. M. NEALE (1818–1866)

❦ Green Grow'th the Holly

Green grow'th the holly,
So doth the ivy;
  Though winter blasts blow ne'er so high,
Green grow'th the holly.

Gay are the flowers,
Hedgerows and ploughlands;
  The days grow longer in the sun,
Soft fall the showers.

Full gold the harvest,
Grain for thy labour;
  With God must work for daily bread,
Else, man, thou starvest.

Fast fall the shed leaves,
Russet and yellow;
  But resting buds are snug and safe
Where swung the dead leaves.

Green grow'th the holly,
So doth the ivy;
  The God of life can never die,
Hope! saith the holly.

ANONYMOUS   97

❧ Greensleeves

The old year now away is fled,
　　The new year it is enterèd;
Then let us now our sins down-tread,
　　And joyfully all appear:
　　　Let's merry be this day,
　　　And let us now both sport and play:
　　　Hang grief, cast care away!
　　　　God send you a happy New Year!

The name-day now of Christ we keep,
　　Who for our sins did often weep;
His hands and feet were wounded deep,
　　And his blessèd side with a spear;
　　　His head they crowned with thorn,
　　　And at him they did laugh and scorn,
　　　Who for our good was born:
　　　　God send us a happy New Year!

And now with New Year's gifts each friend
　　Unto each other they do send:
God grant we may all our lives amend,
　　And that the truth may appear.
　　　Now, like the snake, your skin
　　　Cast off, of evil thoughts and sin,
　　　And so the year begin:
　　　　God send us a happy New Year!

❧ Hark! The Herald Angels Sing

Hark! The Herald Angels Sing,
"Glory to the newborn King!
Peace on earth and mercy mild,
God and sinners reconciled."
Joyful all ye nations rise,
Join the triumph of the skies;
With th'angelic host proclaim,
"Christ is born in Bethlehem."

Hark the Herald Angels Sing,
"Glory to the newborn King!"

Christ, by highest heaven adored;
Christ, the everlasting Lord;
Come, Desire of Nations, come,
Fix in us thy humble home.
Veiled in flesh the Godhead see;
Hail th'Incarnate Deity,
Pleased as man with man to dwell;
Jesus, our Emmanuel.

Hark the Herald Angels Sing,
"Glory to the newborn King!"

continues

CHARLES WESLEY (1707–1788)

Hail, the heave'nborn Prince of Peace!
Hail, the Sun of Righteousness!
Light and life to all He brings,
Ris'n with healing in His wing;
Mild He lays His glory by,
Born that man no more may die,
Born to raise the sons of earth,
Born to give them second birth;

Hark the Herald Angels Sing,
"Glory to the newborn King!"

❧ Here We Come A-Wassailing

Here we come a-wassailing
  Among the leaves so green,
Here we come a-wandering,
  So fair to be seen:

> *Love and joy come to you,*
> *And to you your wassail too,*
> *And God bless you, and send you*
> *A happy new year.*

Our wassail cup is made
  Of the rosemary tree,
And so is your beer
  Of the best barley:

We are not daily beggars
  That beg from door to door,
But we are neighbours' children
  Whom you have seen before:

Call up the butler of this house,
  Put on his golden ring;
Let him bring us up a glass of beer,
  And better we shall sing:

continues

ANONYMOUS

We have got a little purse
    Of stretching leather skin;
We want a little of your money
    To line it well within:

Bring us out a table,
    And spread it with a cloth;
Bring us out a mouldy cheese,
    And some of your Christmas loaf:

God bless the master of this house,
    Likewise the mistress too;
And all the little children
    That round the table go:

Good Master and good Mistress,
    While you're sitting by the fire,
Pray think of us poor children
    Who are wandering in the mire:

Love and joy come to you,
And to you your wassail too,
And God bless you, and send you
A happy new year.

ANONYMOUS

❧ The Holly and the Ivy

The holly and the ivy,
When they are both full grown,
Of all the trees that are in the wood,
The holly bears the crown:

The rising of the sun
And the running of the deer;
The playing of the merry organ,
Sweet singing in the choir.

The holly bears a blossom,
As white as the lily flower,
And Mary bore sweet Jesus Christ,
To be our sweet Saviour:

The holly bears a berry,
As red as any blood,
And Mary bore sweet Jesus Christ
To do poor sinners good:

The holly bears a prickle,
As sharp as any thorn,
And Mary bore sweet Jesus Christ
On Christmas day in the morn:

continues

The holly bears a bark,
As bitter as any gall,
And Mary bore sweet Jesus Christ
For to redeem us all:

The holly and the ivy
When they are both full grown,
Of all the trees that are in the wood,
The holly bears the crown:

*The rising of the sun
And the running of the deer,
The playing of the merry organ,
Sweet singing in the choir.*

ANONYMOUS

❧ The Holy Night

We sate among the stalls at Bethlehem;
The dumb kine from their fodder turning them,
   Softened their hornèd faces
   To almost human gazes
   Toward the newly Born:
The simple shepherds from the star-lit brooks
   Brought visionary looks,
As yet in their astonied hearing rung
   The strange sweet angel-tongue:
The magi of the East, in sandals worn,
   Knelt reverent, sweeping round,
   With long pale beards, their gifts upon the
      ground,
   The incense, myrrh, and gold
These baby hands were impotent to hold:
So let all earthlies and celestials wait
   Upon thy royal state.
   Sleep, sleep, my kingly One!

❧ I Saw Three Ships

I saw three ships come sailing in,
  On Christmas Day, on Christmas Day,
I saw three ships come sailing in,
  On Christmas Day in the morning.

And what was in those ships all three?
  On Christmas Day, on Christmas Day,
And what was in those ships all three?
  On Christmas Day in the morning.

Our Saviour Christ and his lady.
  On Christmas Day, on Christmas Day,
Our Saviour Christ and his lady.
  On Christmas Day in the morning.

Pray, whither sailed those ships all three?
  On Christmas Day, on Christmas Day,
Pray, whither sailed those ships all three?
  On Christmas Day in the morning.

O, they sailed into Bethlehem.
  On Christmas Day, on Christmas Day,
O, they sailed into Bethlehem.
  On Christmas Day in the morning.

　　　　　　　　　ANONYMOUS

And all the bells on earth shall ring,
  On Christmas Day, on Christmas Day,
And all the bells on earth shall ring,
  On Christmas Day in the morning.

And all the angels in Heaven shall sing,
  On Christmas Day, on Christmas Day,
And all the angels in Heaven shall sing,
  On Christmas Day in the morning.

And all the souls on earth shall sing.
  On Christmas Day, on Christmas Day,
And all the souls on earth shall sing.
  On Christmas Day in the morning.

Then let us all rejoice amain!
  On Christmas Day, on Christmas Day,
Then let us all rejoice amain!
  On Christmas Day in the morning.

❧ I Sing of a Maiden

I sing of a maiden
  That is makèless;
King of all kings
  To her son she ches.

He came all so still
  Where his mother was,
As dew in April
  That falleth on the grass.

He came all so still
  To his mother's bowr,
As dew in April
  That falleth on the flower.

He came all so still
  Where his mother lay,
As dew in April
  That falleth on the spray.

Mother and maiden
  Was never none but she;
Well may such a lady
  Godès mother be.

ANONYMOUS

❧ *from* **In Memoriam**

The time draws near the birth of Christ;
   The moon is hid, the night is still;
   A single church below the hill
Is pealing, folded in the mist.

A single peal of bells below,
   That wakens at this hour of rest
   A single murmur in the breast,
That these are not the bells I know.

Like strangers' voices here they sound,
   In lands where not a memory strays,
   Nor landmark breathes of other days,
But all is new unhallow'd ground.

To-night ungather'd let us leave
   This laurel, let this holly stand:
   We live within the stranger's land,
And strangely falls our Christmas-eve.

Our father's dust is left alone
   And silent under other snows:

stanza continues

ALFRED, LORD TENNYSON (1809–1892)   109

There in due time the woodbine blows,
The violet comes, but we are gone.

No more shall wayward grief abuse
   The genial hour with mask and mime;
   For change of place, like growth of time,
Has broke the bond of dying use.

Let cares that petty shadows cast,
   By which our lives are chiefly proved,
   A little spare the night I loved,
And hold it solemn to the past.

But let no footstep beat the floor,
   Nor bowl of wassail mantle warm;
   For who would keep an ancient form
Thro' which the spirit breathes no more?

Be neither song, nor game, nor feast;
   Nor harp be touch'd, nor flute be blown;
   No dance, no motion, save alone
What lightens in the lucid East

Of rising worlds by yonder wood.
   Long sleeps the summer in the seed;
   Run out your measured arcs, and lead
The closing cycle rich in good.

Ring out, wild bells, to the wild sky,
   The flying cloud, the frosty light:
   The year is dying in the night;
Ring out, wild bells, and let him die.

Ring out the old, ring in the new,
   Ring, happy bells, across the snow:
   The year is going, let him go;
Ring out the false, ring in the true.

Ring out the grief that saps the mind,
   For those that here we see no more;
   Ring out the feud of rich and poor,
Ring in redress to all mankind.

Ring out a slowly dying cause,
   And ancient forms of party strife;
   Ring in the nobler modes of life,
With sweeter manners, purer laws.

Ring out the want, the care, the sin,
   The faithless coldness of the times;
   Ring out, ring out my mournful rhymes,
But ring the fuller minstrel in.

continues

Ring out false pride in place and blood,
    The civic slander and the spite;
    Ring in the love of truth and right,
Ring in the common love of good.

Ring out old shapes of foul disease;
    Ring out the narrowing lust of gold;
    Ring out the thousand wars of old,
Ring in the thousand years of peace.

Ring in the valiant man and free,
    The larger heart, the kindlier hand;
    Ring out the darkness of the land,
Ring in the Christ that is to be.

In the Bleak Mid-winter

In the bleak mid-winter
Frosty wind made moan,
Earth stood hard as iron,
Water like a stone;
Snow had fallen, snow on snow,
Snow on snow,
In the bleak mid-winter,
Long ago.

Our God, heav'n cannot hold him
Nor earth sustain;
Heav'n and earth shall flee away
When he comes to reign:
In the bleak mid-winter
A stable-place sufficed
The Lord God Almighty
Jesus Christ.

Enough for him, whom cherubim
Worship night and day,
A breastful of milk,
And a mangerful of hay;
Enough for him, whom angels

stanza continues

Fall down before,
The ox and ass and camel
Which adore.

Angels and archangels
May have gathered there,
Cherubim and seraphim
Thronged the air:
But only his mother
In her maiden bliss
Worshipped the Belovèd
With a kiss.

What can I give him,
Poor as I am?
If I were a shepherd
I would bring a lamb;
If I were a wise man
I would do my part;
Yet what I can I give him—
Give my heart.

❧ It Came Upon the Midnight Clear

It came upon the midnight clear,
That glorious song of old,
From angels bending near the earth
To touch their harps of gold:
"Peace on earth, good will to men,
From heaven's all gracious King."
The world in solemn stillness lay
To hear the angels sing.

Still through the cloven skies they come
With peaceful wings unfurled,
And still their heavenly music floats
O'er all the weary world;
Above its sad and lowly plains
They bend on hovering wing,
And ever o'er its Babel-sounds
The blessed angels sing.

Yet with the woes of sin and strife
The world has suffered long,
Beneath the heavenly hymn have rolled
Two thousand years of wrong;
And warring humankind hears not

stanza continues

EDMUND HAMILTON SEARS (1810–1876)

The tidings which they bring.
O hush the noise and cease your strife
And hear the angels sing.

For lo! The days are hastening on,
By prophets seen of old,
When with the ever-circling years
Shall come the time foretold,
When peace shall over all the earth
Its ancient splendors fling,
And all the world give back the song
Which now the angels sing.

❧ Jest 'Fore Christmas

Father calls me William, sister calls me Will,
Mother calls me Willie, but the fellers call me Bill!
Mighty glad I ain't a girl—ruther be a boy,
Without them sashes, curls, an' things that's worn
   by Fauntleroy!
Love to chawnk green apples an' go swimmin' in
   the lake—
Hate to take the castor-ile they give for belly-ache!
'Most all the time, the whole year round, there ain't
   no flies on me,
But jest 'fore Christmas I'm as good as I kin be!

Got a yeller dog named Sport, sick him on the cat;
First thing she knows she doesn't know where she
   is at!
Got a clipper sled, an' when us kids goes out to slide,
'Long comes the grocery cart, an' we all hook a ride!
But sometimes when the grocery man is worrited
   an' cross,
He reaches at us with his whip, an' larrups up
   his hoss,
An' then I laff an' holler, "Oh, ye never teched *me!*"
But jest 'fore Christmas I'm as good as I kin be!

continues

EUGENE FIELD (1850–1895)

Gran'ma says she hopes that when I git to be a man,
I'll be a missionarer like her oldest brother, Dan,
As was et up by the cannibuls that lives in Ceylon's
  Isle,
Where every prospeck pleases, an' only man is vile!
But gran'ma she has never been to see a Wild West
  show,
Nor read the Life of Daniel Boone, or else I guess
  she'd know
That Buff'lo Bill and cow-boys is good enough
  for me!
Excep' jest 'fore Christmas, when I'm good as I kin be!

And then old Sport he hangs around, so solemn-
  like an' still,
His eyes they keep a-sayin': "What's the matter,
  little Bill?"
The old cat sneaks down off her perch an' wonders
  what's become
Of them two enemies of hern that used to make
  things hum!
But I am so perlite an' 'tend so earnestly to biz,
That mother says to father: "How improved our
  Willie is!"
But father, havin' been a boy hisself, suspicions me
When jest 'fore Christmas, I'm as good as I kin be!

For Christmas, with its lots an' lots of candies,
   cakes an' toys,
Was made, they say, for proper kids an' not for
   naughty boys;
So wash yer face an' bresh yer hair, an' mind yer
   p's an' q's,
An' don't bust out yer pantaloons, an' don't wear
   out yer shoes;
Say "Yessum" to the ladies, an' "Yessur" to
   the men,
An' when they's company, don't pass yer plate for
   pie again;
But, thinking of the things yer'd like to see upon
   that tree,
Jest 'fore Christmas be as good as yer kin be!

❧ Jingle Bells

Dashing thro' the snow in a one-horse open sleigh,
O'er the fields we go, laughing all the way;
Bells on bob-tail ring, making spirits bright;
What fun it is to ride and sing a sleighing song
    tonight!

> *Jingle bells! Jingle bells! Jingle all the way!*
> *Oh! what fun it is to ride in a one-horse open sleigh!*

A day or two ago I thought I'd take a ride,
And soon Miss Fanny Bright was seated by my side;
The horse was lean and lank, misfortunes seemed
    his lot,
He got into a drifted bank, and we got upsot.

> *Jingle bells! Jingle bells! Jingle all the way!*
> *Oh! what fun it is to ride in a one-horse open sleigh!*

Now the ground is white, go it while you're young,
Take the girls tonight, and sing this sleighing song;
Just get a bob-tailed nag, two-forty for his speed,
Then hitch him to an open sleigh, and crack! you'll
    take the lead.

> *Jingle bells! Jingle bells! Jingle all the way!*
> *Oh! what fun it is to ride in a one-horse open sleigh!*

                J. PIERPONT (1822–1893)

❧ Journey of the Magi

"A cold coming we had of it,
Just the worst time of the year
For a journey, and such a long journey:
The ways deep and the weather sharp,
The very dead of winter."
And the camels galled, sore-footed, refractory,
Lying down in the melting snow.
There were times we regretted
The summer palaces on slopes, the terraces,
And the silken girls bringing sherbet.
Then the camel men cursing and grumbling
And running away, and wanting their liquor and
    women,
And the night-fires going out, and the lack of shelters,
And the cities hostile and the towns unfriendly
And the villages dirty and charging high prices:
A hard time we had of it.
At the end we preferred to travel all night,
Sleeping in snatches,
With the voices singing in our ears, saying
That this was all folly.

Then at dawn we came down to a temperate valley,
Wet, below the snow line, smelling of vegetation,

stanza continues

With a running stream and a water-mill beating the
    darkness,
And three trees on the low sky.
And an old white horse galloped away in the meadow.
Then we came to a tavern with vine-leaves over the
    lintel,
Six hands at an open door dicing for pieces of silver,
And feet kicking the empty wine-skins.
But there was no information, and so we continued
And arrived at evening, not a moment too soon
Finding the place; it was (you may say) satisfactory.

All this was a long time ago, I remember,
And I would do it again, but set down
This set down
This: were we led all that way for
Birth or Death? There was a Birth, certainly,
We had evidence and no doubt. I had seen birth
    and death,
But had thought they were different; this Birth was
Hard and bitter agony for us, like Death, our death.
We returned to our places, these Kingdoms,
But no longer at ease here, in the old dispensation,
With an alien people clutching their gods.
I should be glad of another death.

T. S. ELIOT (1888–1965)

❧ Joy to the World

Joy to the world! The Lord is come.
Let Earth receive her King.
Let ev'ry heart prepare Him room,
And Heav'n and Nature sing,
And Heav'n and Nature sing,
And Heav'n, and Heav'n and Nature sing.

Joy to the world! The Savior reigns.
Let men their songs employ,
While fields and floods, rocks, hills, and plains
Repeat the sounding joy,
Repeat the sounding joy,
Repeat, repeat the sounding joy.

He rules the world with truth and grace
And makes the nations prove
The glories of His righteousness
And wonders of His love,
And wonders of His love,
And wonders, wonders of His love.

❧ The Mahogany Tree

Christmas is here:
Winds whistle shrill,
Icy and chill,
Little care we:
Little we fear
Weather without,
Sheltered about
The Mahogany Tree.

Once on the boughs
Birds of rare plume
Sang, in its bloom;
Night-birds are we:
Here we carouse,
Singing like them,
Perched round the stem
Of the jolly old tree.

Here let us sport,
Boys, as we sit;
Laughter and wit
Flashing so free.
Life is but short—

stanza continues

When we are gone,
Let them sing on
Round the old tree.

Evenings we knew,
Happy as this;
Faces we miss,
Pleasant to see.
Kind hearts and true,
Gentle and just,
Peace to your dust!
We sing round the tree.

Care, like a dun,
Lurks at the gate:
Let the dog wait;
Happy we'll be!
Drink, every one;
Pile up the coals,
Fill the red bowls
Round the old tree!

Drain we the cup.—
Friend, art afraid?
Spirits are laid
In the Red Sea.

stanza continues

Mantle it up;
Empty it yet;
Let us forget,
Round the old tree.

Sorrows, begone!
Life and its ills,
Duns and their bills,
Bid we to flee.
Come with the dawn,
Blue-devil sprite,
Leave us to-night
Round the old tree.

❧ The Masque of Christmas

Now God preserve, as you well do deserve,
   Your majesties all two there;
Your highness small, with my good lords all,
   And ladies, how do you do there?

Give me leave to ask, for I bring you a masque
   From little, little, little London;
Which say the king likes, I have passed the pikes,
   If not, old Christmas is undone.

Our dance's freight is a matter of eight,
   And two, the which are wenches:
In all they be ten, four cocks to a hen,
   And will swim to the tune like tenches.

Each hath his knight for to carry his light,
   Which some would say are torches;
To bring them here, and to lead them there,
   And home again to their own porches.

Now their intent, is above to present,
   With all the appurtenances,
A right Christmas, as of old it was,
   To be gathered out of the dances.

continues

Which they do bring, and afore the king,
　　The queen, and prince, as it were now
Drawn here by love; who over and above,
　　Doth draw himself in the gear too.

Hum drum, sauce for a coney;
　　No more of your martial music;
Even for the sake o' the next new stake,
　　For there I do mean to use it.

And now to ye, who in place are to see,
　　With roll and farthingale hoopéd:
I pray you know, though he want his bow,
　　By the wings, that this is Cupid.

He might go back for to cry, What you lack?
　　But that were not so witty:
His cap and coat are enough to note,
　　That he is the Love o' the city.

And he leads on, though he now be gone,
　　For that was only his-rule:
But now comes in, Tom of Bosoms-inn,
　　And he presenteth Mis-rule.

Which you may know, by the very show,
　　Albeit you never ask it:

stanza continues

　　　　　　　BEN JONSON (1572–1637)

For there you may see, what his ensigns be,
  The rope, the cheese, and the basket.

This Carol plays, and has been in his days
  A chirping boy, and a kill-pot:
Kit cobbler it is, I'm a father of his,
  And he dwells in the lane call'd Fill-pot.

But who is this? O, my daughter Cis,
  Minced-pie; with her do not dally
On pain o' your life: she's an honest cook's wife,
  And comes out of Scalding Alley.

Next in the trace, comes Gambol in place:
  And, to make my tale the shorter,
My son Hercules, ta'en out of Distaff Lane,
  But an active man, and a porter.

Now Post and Pair, old Christmas's heir,
  Doth make and a jingling sally;
And wot you who, 'tis one of my two
  Sons, card-makers in Pur Alley.

Next in a trice, with his box and his dice,
  Mac'-pipin my son, but younger,
Brings Mumming in; and the knave will win,
  For he is a costermonger.

continues

But New Year's Gift, of himself makes shift,
    To tell you what his name is:
With orange on head, and his ginger-bread,
    Clem Wasp of Honey Lane 'tis.

This, I you tell, is our jolly Wassel,
    And for Twelfth-night more meet too:
She works by the ell, and her name is Nell,
    And she dwells in Threadneedle Street too.

Then Offering, he, with his dish and his tree,
    That in every great house keepeth,
Is by my son, young Little-worth, done,
    And in Penny-rich Street he sleepeth.

Last, Baby-cake, that an end doth make
    Of Christmas' merry, merry vein-a,
Is child Rowlan, and a straight young man,
    Though he come out of Crooked Lane-a.

There should have been, and a dozen I ween,
    But I could find but one more
Child of Christmas, and a Log it was,
    When I them all had gone o'er.

I prayéd him, in a time so trim,
    That he would make one to prance it:
And I myself would have been the twelfth,
    O but Log was too heavy to dance it.

❧ "Men may talk of country-Christmasses and court-gluttony,"

Men may talk of country-Christmasses and
    court-gluttony,
Their thirty-pound buttered eggs, their pies
    of carps' tongues,
Their pheasants drenched with ambergris,
    the carcases
Of three fat wethers bruised for gravy, to
Make sauce for a single peacock; yet their feasts
Were fasts, compared with the city's . . .

Did you not observe it?
There were three sucking pigs served up in a dish,
Ta'en from the sow as soon as farrowed,
A fortnight fed with dates, and muskadine,
That stood my master in twenty marks apiece,
Besides the puddings in their bellies, made
Of I know not what.—I dare swear the cook that
    dressed it
Was the devil, disguised like a Dutchman.

The Mistletoe

'Neath mistletoe, should chance arise,
You may be happy if you're wise.
Though bored you lie with pantomime
And Christmas fare and Christmas rhyme —
One fine old custom don't despise.

If you're a man of enterprise,
You'll find, I venture to surmise,
'Tis pleasant then at Christmas time
        'Neath mistletoe!

You see they scarcely can disguise
The sparkle of their pretty eyes;
And no one thinks it is a crime,
When goes the merry Christmas chime,
A rare old rite to exercise
        'Neath mistletoe!

J. ASHBY-STERRY (1838–1865)

∾ Nativity

Immensity cloistered in thy dear womb,
Now leaves his well-beloved imprisonment,
There he hath made himself to his intent
Weak enough, now into our world to come;
But Oh, for thee, for him, hath th' Inn no room?
Yet lay him in this stall, and from the Orient,
Stars, and wisemen will travel to prevent
Th' effect of Herod's jealous general doom.
Seest thou, my Soul, with thy faith's eyes, how he
Which fills all place, yet none holds him, doth lie?
Was not his pity towards thee wondrous high,
That would have need to be pitied by thee?
Kiss him, and with him into Egypt go,
With his kind mother, who partakes thy woe.

❧ The Nativity

Peace? and to all the world? sure, one
And he the prince of peace, hath none.
He travels to be born, and then
Is born to travel more agen.
Poor *Galile!* thou can'st not be
The place for his Nativity.
His restless mother's call'd away,
And not deliver'd till she pay.

   A *Tax?* 'tis so still! we can see
The Church thrive in her misery;
And like her head at *Bethlem*, rise
When she opprest with troubles, lyes.
Rise? should all fall, we cannot be
In more extremities than he.
Great *Type* of passions! come what will,
Thy grief exceeds all *copies* still.
Thou cam'st from heav'n to earth, that we
Might go from Earth to Heav'n with thee.
And though thou found'st no welcom here,
Thou did'st provide us *mansions* there.
A *stable* was thy *Court,* and when
Men turn'd to *beasts*; Beasts would be *Men.*
They were thy *Courtiers,* others none;
And their poor *Manger* was thy *Throne.*

continues

No swadling *silks* thy Limbs did fold,
Though thou could'st turn thy Rays to gold.
No *Rockers* waited on thy birth,
No *Cradles* stirr'd: nor songs of mirth;
But her chast *Lap* and sacred *Brest*
Which lodg'd thee first, did give thee *rest*.
   But stay: what light is that doth stream,
And drop here in a gilded beam?
It is thy Star runs *page,* and brings
Thy tributary *Eastern* Kings.
Lord! grant some *Light* to us, that we
May with them find the way to thee.
Behold what mists eclipse the day:
How dark it is! shed down one *Ray*
To guide us out of this sad night,
And say once more, *Let there be Light.*

❧ The Nativity of Our Lord and Saviour Jesus Christ

Where is this stupendous stranger?
    Swains of Solyma, advise;
Lead me to my Master's manger,
    Shew me where my Saviour lies.

O Most Mighty! O Most Holy!
    Far beyond the seraph's thought,
Art thou then so mean and lowly
    As unheeded prophets taught?

O the magnitude of meekness!
    Worth from worth immortal sprung;
O the strength of infant weakness,
    If eternal is so young!

If so young and thus eternal,
    Michael tune the shepherd's reed,
Where the scenes are ever vernal,
    And the loves be love indeed!

See the God blasphem'd and doubted
    In the schools of Greece and Rome;
See the pow'rs of darkness routed,
    Taken at their utmost gloom.

continues

CHRISTOPHER SMART (1722–1771)   137

Nature's decorations glisten
　　Far above their usual trim;
Birds on box and laurels listen,
　　As so near the cherubs hymn.

Boreas now no longer winters
　　On the desolated coast;
Oaks no more are riv'n in splinters
　　By the whirlwind and his host.

Spinks and ouzles sing sublimely,
　　"We too have a Saviour born";
Whiter blossoms burst untimely
　　On the blest Mosaic thorn.

God all-bounteous, all-creative,
　　Whom no ills from good dissuade,
Is incarnate, and a native
　　Of the very world he made.

❧ New Prince, New Pomp

Behold, a silly tender Babe
   In freezing winter night
In homely manger trembling lies,
   Alas, a piteous sight!

The inns are full; no man will yield
   This little pilgrim bed,
But forced he is with silly beasts
   In crib to shroud his head.

Despise him not for lying there,
   First, what he is inquire;
An orient pearl is often found
   In depth of dirty mire.

Weigh not his crib, his wooden dish,
   Nor beasts that by him feed;
Weigh not his Mother's poor attire,
   Nor Joseph's simple weed.

This stable is a Prince's court,
   This crib his chair of state;
The beasts are parcel of his pomp,
   The wooden dish his plate.

continues

ROBERT SOUTHWELL (1561–1595)   139

The persons in that poor attire
    His royal liveries wear;
The Prince himself is come from heaven;
    This pomp is prized there.

With joy approach, O Christian wight,
    Do homage to thy King;
And highly praise his humble pomp,
    Which he from heaven doth bring.

❧ Now Thrice Welcome Christmas

from *POOR ROBIN'S ALMANACK*

Now thrice welcome Christmas,
    Which brings us good-cheer,
Minced pies and plum-porridge,
    Good ale and strong beer;
With pig, goose, and capon,
    The best that can be,
So well doth the weather
    And our stomachs agree.

Observe how the chimneys
    Do smoke all about,
The cooks are providing
    For dinner no doubt;
But those on whose tables
    No victuals appear,
O may they keep Lent
    All the rest of the year!

With holly and ivy
    So green and so gay,
We deck up our houses
    As fresh as the day,
With bays and rosemary,
    And laurel complete,
And everyone now
    Is a king in conceit.

TRADITIONAL SONG

❧ O Christmas Tree

(O Tannenbaum)

O Christmas tree, O Christmas tree,
With faithful leaves unchanging.
Not only green in summer's heat,
But also winter's snow and sleet.
O Christmas tree, O Christmas tree,
With faithful leaves unchanging.

O Christmas tree, O Christmas tree,
Of all the trees most lovely;
Each year, you bring to me delight
Gleaming in the Christmas night.
O Christmas tree, O Christmas tree,
Of all the trees most lovely.

O Christmas tree, O Christmas tree,
Your leaves will teach me, also,
That hope and love and faithfulness
Are precious things I can possess.
O Christmas tree, O Christmas tree,
Your leaves will teach me, also.

❧ O Come, All Ye Faithful

O come, all ye faithful,
Joyful and triumphant;
O come ye, O come ye to Bethlehem;
Come and behold Him
Born the King of angels;

O come, let us adore Him,
O come, let us adore Him,
O come, let us adore Him,
Christ the Lord.

Sing, choirs of angels,
Sing in exultation,
Sing all ye citizens of heav'n above:
Glory to God
In the highest.

O come, let us adore Him,
O come, let us adore Him,
O come, let us adore Him,
Christ the Lord.

Yea Lord, we greet Thee,
Born this happy morning;

stanza continues

Jesus to Thee be glory giv'n;
Word of the Father,
Now in flesh appearing.

O come, let us adore Him,
O come, let us adore Him,
O come, let us adore Him,
Christ the Lord.

O Holy Night

O Holy Night! The stars are brightly shining,
It is the night of our dear savior's birth;
Long lay the world in sin and error pining,
Till He appeared and the soul felt its worth.

A thrill of hope the weary soul rejoices,
For yonder breaks a new and glorious morn;
Fall on your knees! Oh, hear the angel voices!
O night divine! O night when Christ was born!
O night, O holy night, O night divine.

O Little Town of Bethlehem

O little town of Bethlehem,
  How still we see thee lie!
Above thy deep and dreamless sleep
  The silent stars go by.
Yet in thy dark streets shineth
  The everlasting light;
The hopes and fears of all the years
  Are met in thee to-night.

O morning stars, together
  Proclaim the holy birth,
And praises sing to God the King,
  And peace to men on earth;
For Christ is born of Mary;
  And, gathered all above,
While mortals sleep, the angels keep
  Their watch of wondering love.

How silently, how silently,
  The wondrous gift is given!
So God imparts to human hearts
  The blessings of his heaven.
No ear may hear his coming;
  But in this world of sin,
Where meek souls will receive him, still
  The dear Christ enters in.

PHILLIPS BROOKS (1835–1893)

Where children pure and happy
    Pray to the blessèd Child,
Where misery cries out to thee,
    Son of the mother mild;
Where charity stands watching
    And faith holds wide the door,
The dark night wakes, the glory breaks,
    And Christmas comes once more.

O holy Child of Bethlehem,
    Descend to us, we pray;
Cast out our sin, and enter in,
    Be born in us to-day.
We hear the Christmas Angels
    The great glad tidings tell:
O come to us, abide with us,
    Our Lord Emmanuel.

❧ An Ode of the Birth of Our Saviour

In Numbers, and but these few,
I sing Thy Birth, Oh JESU!
Thou prettie Babie, borne here,
With sup'rabundant scorn here:
Who for Thy Princely Port here,
    Hadst for Thy place
    Of Birth, a base
Out-stable for thy Court here.

Instead of neat Inclosures
Of inter-woven Osiers;
Instead of fragrant Posies
Of Daffadills, and Roses;
Thy cradle, Kingly Stranger,
    As Gospell tells,
    Was nothing els,
But, here, a homely manger.

But we with Silks, (not Cruells)
With sundry precious Jewells,
And Lilly-work will dresse Thee;
And as we dispossesse thee

stanza continues

148   ROBERT HERRICK (1591–1674)

Of clouts, wee'l make a chamber,
    Sweet Babe, for Thee,
    Of Ivorie,
And plaister'd round with Amber.

The Jewes they did disdaine Thee,
But we will entertaine Thee
With Glories to await here
Upon Thy Princely State here,
And more for love, then pittie.
    From yeere to yeere
    Wee'l make Thee, here,
A Free-born of our Citie.

❧ Old Christmastide

Heap on more wood! —the wind is chill;
But let it whistle as it will,
We'll keep our Christmas merry still.
Each age has deemed the new-born year
The fittest time for festal cheer.
Even heathen yet, the savage Dane
At Iol more deep the mead did drain;
High on the beach his galley drew,
And feasted all his pirate crew;
Then in his low and pine-built hall,
Where shields and axes decked the wall,
They gorged upon the half-dressed steer;
Caroused in seas of sable beer;
While round, in brutal jest, were thrown
The half-gnawed rib and marrow-bone,
Or listened all, in grim delight,
While scalds yelled out the joy of fight,
Then forth in frenzy would they hie,
While wildly loose their red locks fly;
And, dancing round the blazing pile,
They make such barbarous mirth the while,
As best might to the mind recall
The boisterous joys of Odin's hall.
And well our Christian sire of old
Loved when the year its course had rolled,

And brought blithe Christmas back again,
With all his hospitable train.
Domestic and religious rite
Gave honour to the holy night:
On Christmas eve the bells were rung;
On Christmas eve the mass was sung;
That only night, in all the year,
Saw the stoled priest the chalice rear.
The damsel donned her kirtle sheen;
The hall was dressed with holly green;
Forth to the wood did merry men go,
To gather in the mistletoe;
Then opened wide the baron's hall
To vassal, tenant, serf, and all;
Power laid his rod of rule aside,
And ceremony doffed his pride.
The heir, with roses in his shoes,
That night might village partner choose;
The lord, underogating, share
The vulgar game of "post and pair."
All hailed, with uncontrolled delight,
And general voice, the happy night
That to the cottage, as the crown,
Brought tidings of salvation down.
The fire, with well-dried logs supplied,
Went roaring up the chimney wide;

continues

SIR WALTER SCOTT (1771–1832)

The huge hall-table's oaken face,
Scrubbed till it shone, the day to grace,
Bore then upon its massive board
No mark to part the squire and lord.
Then was brought in the lusty brawn
By old blue-coated serving man;
Then the grim boar's head frowned on high,
Crested with bays and rosemary.
Well can the green-garbed ranger tell,
How, when, and where the monster fell;
What dogs before his death he tore,
And all the baiting of the boar.
The Wassail round, in good brown bowls,
Garnished with ribbons, blithely trowls.
There the huge sirloin reeked; hard by
Plum-porridge stood, and Christmas pie;
Nor failed old Scotland to produce,
At such high tide, her savoury goose.
Then came the merry masquers in,
And carols roared with blithesome din;
If unmelodious was the song,
It was a hearty note, and strong,
Who lists may in their mumming see
Traces of ancient mystery;
White shirts supplied the masquerade,
And smutted cheeks the vizors made:
But, what masquers, richly dight,
Can boast of bosoms half so light?

England was merry England, when
Old Christmas brought his sports again.
'Twas Christmas broached the mightiest ale;
'Twas Christmas told the merriest tale;
A Christmas gambol oft could cheer
The poor man's heart through half the year.

❧ On Christmas Day to My Heart

To Day:
Hark! Heaven sings!
Stretch, tune my Heart
(For hearts have strings
May bear their part)
And though thy Lute were bruis'd i' th' fall;
Bruis'd hearts may reach an humble Partoral.

To Day
Shepheards rejoyce
And Angells do
No more: thy voice
Can reach that too:
Bring then at least thy pipe along
And mingle Consort with the Angells Song.

To Day
A shed that's thatch'd
(Yet straws can sing)
Holds God; God's match'd
With beasts; Beasts bring
Their song their way; For shame then raise
Thy notes; Lambs bleat and Oxen bellow Praise.

To Day
God honour'd Man
Not Angells: Yet
They sing; And can
Rais'd Man forget?
Praise is our debt to-day, nor shall
Angells (Man's not so poor) discharge it all.

To Day
Then screwe thee high
My Heart: Up to
The Angells key;
Sing Glory; Do;
What if thy stringes all crack and flye?
On such a Ground, Musick 'twill be to dy.

❧ On the Infancy of Our Savior

Hail! blessed Virgin, full of heavenly grace,
Blest above all that sprang from human race,
Whose heaven-saluted womb brought forth in one
A blessed Savior and a blessed Son.
O what a ravishment 't had been to see
Thy little Savior perking on thy knee!
To see Him nuzzle in thy virgin breast,
His milk-white body all unclad, undressed;
To see thy busy fingers clothe and wrap
His spraddling limbs in thy indulgent lap;
To see His desperate eyes with childish grace
Smiling upon His smiling mother's face;
And when His forward strength began to bloom
To see Him diddle up and down the room.
O who would think so sweet a Babe as this
Should ere be slain by a false-hearted kiss?
Had I a rag, if sure Thy body wore it,
Pardon, sweet Babe, I think I should adore it,
Till then, O grant this boon, a boon far dearer:
The weed not being, I may adore the Wearer.

FRANCIS QUARLES (1592–1644)

❧ On the Morning of Christ's Nativity

This is the month, and this the happy morn
Wherein the Son of Heaven's Eternal King,
Of wedded maid and virgin mother born,
Our great redemption from above did bring;
For so the holy sages once did sing
That he our deadly forfeit should release,
And with his Father work us a perpetual peace.

That glorious Form, that Light unsufferable,
And that far-beaming blaze of Majesty
Wherewith he wont at Heaven's high council-ta
To sit the midst of Trinal Unity,
He laid aside; and, here with us to be,
Forsook the courts of everlasting day,
And chose with us a darksome house of mortal clay.

Say, Heavenly Muse, shall not thy sacred vein
Afford a present to the Infant God?
Hast thou no verse, no hymn, or solemn strain
To welcome him to this his new abode,
Now while the heaven, by the sun's team untrod,
Hath took no print of the approaching light,
And all the spangled host keep watch in squadrons
  bright?

continues

JOHN MILTON (1608–1674)   157

See how from far, upon the eastern road,
The star-led wizards haste with odors sweet!
O run, prevent them with thy humble ode
And lay it lowly at his blessed feet;
Have thou the honor first thy Lord to greet,
And join thy voice unto the angel choir
From out his secret altar touched with hallowed fire.

The Hymn

It was the winter wild
While the heaven-born Child
All meanly wrapped in the rude manger lies;
Nature in awe to Him
Had doffed her gaudy trim,
With her great Master so to sympathize:
It was no season then for her
To wanton with the sun, her lusty paramour.

Only with speeches fair
She woos the gentle air
To hide her guilty front with innocent snow;
And on her naked shame,
Pollute with sinful blame,
The saintly veil of maiden white to throw;
Confounded, that her Maker's eyes
Should look so near upon her foul deformities.

JOHN MILTON (1608–1674)

But he, her fears to cease,
Sent down the meek-eyed Peace;
She, crowned with olive green, came softly sliding
Down through the turning sphere,
His ready harbinger,
With turtle wing and amorous clouds dividing;
And waving wide her myrtle wand,
She strikes a universal peace through sea and land.

No war, or battle's sound
Was heard the world around:
The idle spear and shield were high uphung;
The hookèd chariot stood
Unstained with hostile blood;
The trumpet spake not to the armèd throng;
And kings sat still with awful eye,
As if they surely knew their sovereign Lord was by.

But peaceful was the night
Wherein the Prince of Light
His reign of peace upon the earth began:
The winds, with wonder whist,
Smoothly the waters kissed,
Whispering new joys to the mild oceàn—
Who now hath quite forgot to rave,
While birds of calm sit brooding on the charmèd wave.

continues

The stars, with deep amaze,
Stand fixed in steadfast gaze,
Bending one way their precious influence;
And will not take their flight
For all the morning light,
Or Lucifer that often warned them thence;
But in their glimmering orbs did glow
Until their Lord himself bespake, and bid them go.

And though the shady gloom
Had given day her room,
The sun himself withheld his wonted speed,
And hid his head for shame,
As his inferior flame
The new-enlightened world no more should need;
He saw a greater Sun appear
Than his bright throne, or burning axletree,
    could bear.

The shepherds on the lawn
Or ere the point of dawn
Sat simply chatting in a rustic row;
Full little thought they then
That the mighty Pan
Was kindly come to live with them below;
Perhaps their loves, or else their sheep,
Was all that did their silly thoughts so busy keep.

When such music sweet
Their hearts and ears did greet
As never was by mortal finger strook —
Divinely-warbled voice
Answering the stringèd noise,
As all their souls in blissful rapture took:
The air, such pleasure loth to lose,
With thousand echoes still prolongs each
    heavenly close.

Nature, that heard such sound
Beneath the hollow round
Of Cynthia's seat the airy region thrilling,
Now was almost won
To think her part was done,
And that her reign had here its last fulfilling;
She knew such harmony alone
Could hold all heaven and earth in happier union.

At last surrounds their sight
A globe of circular light
That with long beams the shamefaced night arrayed;
The helmèd Cherubim
And sworded Seraphim
Are seen in glittering ranks with wings displayed,
Harping in loud and solemn choir
With unexpressive notes, to Heaven's new-born Heir.

continues

JOHN MILTON (1608–1674)   161

Such music (as 'tis said)
Before was never made
But when of old the sons of morning sung,
While the Creator great
His constellations set
And the well-balanced world on hinges hung;
And cast the dark foundations deep,
And bid the weltering waves their oozy channel keep.

Ring out, ye crystal spheres!
Once bless our human ears,
If ye have power to touch our senses so;
And let your silver chime
Move in melodious time;
And let the bass of Heaven's deep organ blow;
And with your ninefold harmony
Make up full consort to the angelic symphony.

For if such holy song
Enwrap our fancy long,
Time will run back, and fetch the age of gold;
And speckled vanity
Will sicken soon and die,
And leprous sin will melt from earthly mould;
And Hell itself will pass away,
And leave her dolorous mansions to the peering day.

JOHN MILTON (1608–1674)

Yea, Truth and Justice then
Will down return to men,
Orbed in a rainbow; and, like glories wearing,
Mercy will sit between
Throned in celestial sheen,
With radiant feet the tissued clouds down steering;
And Heaven, as at some festival,
Will open wide the gates of her high palace hall.

But wisest Fate says No;
This must not yet be so;
The Babe yet lies in smiling infancy
That on the bitter cross
Must redeem our loss;
So both himself and us to glorify:
Yet first, to those ychained in sleep
The wakeful trump of doom must thunder through
    the deep;

With such a horrid clang
As on Mount Sinai rang
While the red fire and smouldering clouds outbrake:
The agèd Earth aghast
With terror of that blast
Shall from the surface to the centre shake,

stanza continues

When, at the world's last sessiòn,
The dreadful Judge in middle air shall spread
  His throne.

And then at last our bliss
Full and perfect is,
But now begins; for from this happy day
The old Dragon under ground,
In straiter limits bound,
Not half so far casts his usurpèd sway;
And, wroth to see his kingdom fail,
Swinges the scaly horror of his folded tail.

The oracles are dumb;
No voice or hideous hum
Runs through the archèd roof in words deceiving.
Apollo from his shrine
Can no more divine,
With hollow shriek the steep of Delphos leaving:
No nightly trance or breathèd spell
Inspires the pale-eyed priest from the prophetic cell.

The lonely mountains o'er
And the resounding shore
A voice of weeping heard, and loud lament;
From haunted spring and dale
Edged with poplar pale

stanza continues

The parting Genius is with sighing sent;
With flower-inwoven tresses torn
The Nymphs in twilight shade of tangled thickets
    mourn.

In consecrated earth
And on the holy hearth
The Lars and Lemures moan with midnight plaint;
In urns, and altars round
A drear and dying sound
Affrights the Flamens at their service quaint;
And the chill marble seems to sweat,
While each peculiar Power foregoes his wonted seat.

Peor and Baälim
Forsake their temples dim,
With that twice-battered god of Palestine;
And moonèd Ashtaroth
Heaven's queen and mother both,
Now sits not girt with tapers' holy shine;
The Lybic Hammon shrinks his horn:
In vain the Tyrian maids their wounded
    Thammuz mourn.

And sullen Moloch, fled,
Hath left in shadows dread

stanza continues

His burning idol all of blackest hue;
In vain with cymbals' ring
They call the grisly king,
In dismal dance about the furnace blue;
The brutish gods of Nile as fast,
Isis, and Orus, and the dog Anubis, haste.

Nor is Osiris seen
In Memphian grove, or green,
Trampling the unshowered grass with lowings loud:
Nor can he be at rest
Within his sacred chest;
Naught but profoundest Hell can be his shroud;
In vain with timbrelled anthems dark
The sable stolèd sorcerers bear his worshiped ark.

He feels from Juda's land
The dreaded Infant's hand;
The rays of Bethlehem blind his dusky eyen;
Nor all the gods beside
Longer dare abide
Nor Typhon huge ending in snaky twine:
Our Babe, to show his Godhead true,
Can in His swaddling bands control the
    damnèd crew.

So, when the sun in bed
Curtained with cloudy red
Pillows his chin upon an orient wave,
The flocking shadows pale
Troop to the infernal jail,
Each fettered ghost slips to his several grave:
And the yellow-skirted fays
Fly after the night-steeds, leaving their moon-
    loved maze.

But see! the Virgin blest
Hath laid her Babe to rest;
Time is, our tedious song should here have ending:
Heaven's youngest teemèd star
Hath fixed her polished car,
Her sleeping Lord with hand-maid lamp attending:
And all about the courtly stable
Bright-harnessed Angels sit in order serviceable.

❧ The Oxen

Christmas Eve, and twelve of the clock.
  "Now they are all on their knees,"
An elder said as we sat in a flock
  By the embers in hearthside ease.

We pictured the meek mild creatures where
  They dwelt in their strawy pen,
Nor did it occur to one of us there
  To doubt they were kneeling then.

So fair a fancy few would weave
  In these years! Yet, I feel,
If someone said on Christmas Eve,
  "Come; see the oxen kneel

"In the lonely barton by yonder coomb
  Our childhood used to know,"
I should go with him in the gloom,
  Hoping it might be so.

❧ Presents

I wanted a rifle for Christmas,
   I wanted a bat and a ball,
I wanted some skates and a bicycle,
   But I didn't want mittens at all.

   I wanted a whistle
     And I wanted a kite.
   I wanted a pocketknife
     That shut up tight.
   I wanted some boots
     And I wanted a kit,
But I didn't want mittens one little bit.

I told them I didn't like mittens,
   I told them as plain as plain.
I told them I didn't WANT mittens,
   And they've given me mittens again!

MARCHETTE CHUTE (1909–1994)

❧ The Reminder

While I watch the Christmas blaze
Paint the room with ruddy rays,
Something makes my vision glide
To the frosty scene outside.

There, to reach a rotting berry,
Toils a thrush—constrained to very
Dregs of food by sharp distress,
Taking such with thankfulness.

Why, O starving bird, when I
One day's joy would justify,
And put misery out of view,
Do you make me notice you?

❧ Rudolph the Red-Nosed Reindeer

You know Dasher and Dancer
  And Prancer and Vixen,
Comet and Cupid
  And Donner and Blitzen,
But do you recall
  The most famous reindeer of all?

Rudolph, the Red-Nosed Reindeer
  Had a very shiny nose,
And if you ever saw it,
  You would even say it glows.

All of the other reindeer
  Used to laugh and call him names,
They never let poor Rudolph
  Join in any reindeer games.

Then one foggy Christmas Eve,
  Santa came to Say,
"Rudolph, with your nose so bright,
  Won't you guide my sleigh tonight?"

Then how the reindeer loved him
  As they shouted out with glee:
"Rudolph, the Red-Nosed Reindeer,
  You'll go down in history!"

JOHNNY MARKS (1909–1985)

The Shepherd Who Stayed

There are in Paradise
Souls neither great nor wise,
Yet souls who wear no less
The crown of faithfulness.

My master bade me watch the flock by night;
My duty was to stay. I do not know
What thing my comrades saw in that great light,
I did not heed the words that bade them go,
I know not were they maddened or afraid;
   I only know I stayed.

The hillside seemed on fire; I felt the sweep
Of wings above my head; I ran to see
If any danger threatened these my sheep.
What though I found them folded quietly,
What though my brother wept and plucked my
   sleeve,
   They were not mine to leave.

Thieves in the wood and wolves upon the hill,
My duty was to stay. Strange though it be,
I had no thought to hold my mates, no will
To bid them wait and keep the watch with me.
I had not heard that summons they obeyed;
   I only know I stayed.

THEODOSIA GARRISON (1874–1944)

Perchance they will return upon the dawn
With word of Bethlehem and why they went.
I only know that watching here alone,
I know a strange content.
I have not failed that trust upon me laid;
    I ask no more — I stayed.

ᔌ "Shut in from all the world without,"

from *SNOW-BOUND*

Shut in from all the world without,
We sat the clean-winged hearth about,
Content to let the north-wind roar
In baffled rage at pane and door,
While the red logs before us beat
The frost-line back with tropic heat;
And ever, when a louder blast
Shook beam and rafter as it passed,
The merrier up its roaring draught
The great throat of the chimney laughed.

❧ Silent Night

Silent Night, holy night,
All is calm, all is bright.
'Round yon virgin mother and child.
Holy infant so tender and mild,
Sleep in heavenly peace,
Sleep in heavenly peace.

Silent night! Holy night!
Shepherds quake at the sight!
Glories stream from Heaven afar,
Heav'nly hosts sing Alleluia,
Christ, the Saviour, is born!
Christ, the Saviour, is born!

Silent night! Holy night!
Son of God, love's pure light,
Radiant beams from Thy holy face,
With the dawn of redeeming grace,
Jesus, Lord, at Thy birth,
Jesus, Lord, at Thy birth.

❧ Skating

And in the frosty season, when the sun
Was set, and visible for many a mile
The cottage windows blazed through twilight gloom,
I heeded not their summons: happy time
It was indeed for all of us—for me
It was a time of rapture! Clear and loud
The village clock tolled six,—I wheeled about
Proud and exulting like an untired horse
That cares not for his home. All shod with steel,
We hissed along the polished ice in games
Confederate, imitative of the chase
And woodland pleasures,—the resounding horn,
The pack loud chiming, and the hunted hare.

✒ Sly Santa Claus

All the house was asleep,
    And the fire burning low,
When, from far up the chimney,
    Came down a "Ho! ho!"
And a little, round man,
    With a terrible scratching,
Dropped into the room
    With a wink that was catching.
Yes, down he came, bumping,
And thumping, and jumping,
    And picking himself up without sign of a bruise!

"Ho! ho!" he kept on,
    As if bursting with cheer.
"Good children, gay children,
    Glad children, see here!
I have brought you fine dolls,
    And gay trumpets, and rings,
Noah's arks, and bright skates,
    And a host of good things!
I have brought a whole sackful,
A packful, a hackful!
    Come hither, come hither, come hither and choose!

continues

"Ho! ho! What is this?
    Why, they all are asleep!
But their stockings are up,
    And my presents will keep!
So, in with the candies,
    The books, and the toys;
All the goodies I have
    For the good girls and boys.
I'll ram them, and jam them,
And slam them, and cram them;
    All the stockings will hold while the tired
        youngsters snooze."

All the while his round shoulders
    Kept ducking and ducking;
And his little, fat fingers
    Kept tucking and tucking;
Until every stocking
    Bulged out, on the wall,
As if it were bursting,
    And ready to fall.
And then, all at once,
    With a whisk and a whistle,
And twisting himself
    Like a tough bit of gristle,
He bounced up again,
    Like the down of a thistle,
        And nothing was left but the prints of his shoes.

❧ The Snow-man

Look! how the clouds are flying south!
  The wind pipes loud and shrill!
And high above the white drifts stands
  The snow-man on the hill.

Blow, wild wind from the icy north!
  Here's one who will not fear
To feel thy coldest touch, or shrink
  Thy loudest blast to hear!

Proud triumph of the school-boy's skill!
  Far rather would I be
A winter giant, ruling o'er
  A frosty realm, like thee,

And stand amidst the drifted snow,
  Like thee, a thing apart,
Than be a man who walks with men,
  But has a frozen heart!

MARIAN DOUGLAS (1842–1913)

❧ The Snowstorm

Announced by all the trumpets of the sky,
Arrives the snow, and, driving o'er the fields,
Seems nowhere to alight: the whited air
Hides hills and woods, the river, and the heaven,
And veils the farmhouse at the garden's end.
The sled and traveler stopped, the courier's feet
Delayed, all friends shut out, the housemates sit
Around the radiant fireplace, enclosed
In a tumultuous privacy of storm.

Come, see the north wind's masonry.
Out of an unseen quarry evermore
Furnished with tile, the fierce artificer
Curves his white bastions with projected roof
Round every windward stake or tree or door.
Speeding, the myriad-handed, his wild work
So fanciful, so savage, naught cares he
For number or proportion. Mockingly
On coop or kennel he hangs Parian wreaths;
A swan-like form invests the hidden thorn;
Fills up the farmer's lane from wall to wall,
Maugre the farmer's sighs; and at the gate
A tapering turret overtops the work.
And when his hours are numbered, and the world

stanza continues

RALPH WALDO EMERSON (1803–1882)

Is all his own, retiring, as he were not,
Leaves, when the sun appears, astonished Art
To mimic in slow structures, stone by stone,
Built in an age, the mad wind's night-work,
The frolic architecture of the snow.

Song

Why do bells for Christmas ring?
Why do little children sing?

Once a lovely, shining star,
Seen by shepherds from afar,
Gently moved until its light
Made a manger's cradle bright.

There a darling baby lay,
Pillowed soft upon the hay;
And its mother sang and smiled,
"This is Christ, the holy child!"

Therefore bells for Christmas ring,
Therefore little children sing.

EUGENE FIELD (1850–1895)

"There were in the same country shepherds abiding in the field,"

from *LUKE*

There were in the same country shepherds abiding
  in the field, keeping watch over their flock by
  night.
And, lo, the angel of the Lord came upon them, and
  the glory of the Lord shone round about them:
  and they were sore afraid.
And the angel said unto them, Fear not, for behold,
  I bring you good tidings of great joy, which shall
  be to all people.
For unto you is born this day in the city of David, a
  Saviour, which is Christ the Lord.
And this *shall be* a sign unto you; Ye shall find the
  babe wrapped in swaddling clothes, lying in a
  manger.
And suddenly there was with the angel a multitude
  of the heav'nly host, praising God, and saying,
Glory to God in the highest, and on earth peace,
  good will toward men.

❧ The Three Kings

Three Kings came riding from far away,
  Melchior and Gaspar and Baltasar;
Three Wise Men out of the East were they,
And they travelled by night and they slept by day,
  For their guide was a beautiful, wonderful star.

The star was so beautiful, large, and clear,
  That all the other stars of the sky
Became a white mist in the atmosphere,
And by this they knew that the coming was near
  Of the Prince foretold in the prophecy.

Three caskets they bore on their saddle-bows,
  Three caskets of gold with golden keys;
Their robes were of crimson silk with rows
Of bells and pomegranates and furbelows,
  Their turbans like blossoming almond-trees.

And so the Three Kings rode into the West,
  Through the dusk of night, over hill and dell,
And sometimes they nodded with beard on breast,
And sometimes talked, as they paused to rest,
  With the people they met at some wayside well.

"Of the child that is born," said Baltasar,
    "Good people, I pray you, tell us the news;
For we in the East have seen his star,
And have ridden fast, and have ridden far,
    To find and worship the King of the Jews."

And the people answered, "You ask in vain;
    We know of no king but Herod the Great!"
They thought the Wise Men were men insane,
As they spurred their horses across the plain,
    Like riders in haste, and who cannot wait.

And when they came to Jerusalem,
    Herod the Great, who had heard this thing,
Sent for the Wise Men and questioned them;
And said, "Go down unto Bethlehem,
    And bring me tidings of this new king."

So they rode away; and the star stood still,
    The only one in the gray of morn;
Yes, it stopped,—it stood still of its own free will,
Right over Bethlehem on the hill,
    The city of David, where Christ was born.

And the Three Kings rode through the gate and
    the guard,
    Through the silent street, till their horses turned

stanza continues

And neighed as they entered the great inn-yard;
But the windows were closed, and the doors
        were barred,
    And only a light in the stable burned.

And cradled there in the scented hay,
    In the air made sweet by the breath of kine,
The little child in the manger lay,
The child, that would be king one day
    Of a kingdom not human but divine.

His mother Mary of Nazareth
    Sat watching beside his place of rest,
Watching the even flow of his breath,
For the joy of life and the terror of death
    Were mingled together in her breast.

They laid their offerings at his feet:
    The gold was their tribute to a King,
The frankincense, with its odor sweet,
Was for the Priest, the Paraclete,
    The myrhh for the body's burying.

And the mother wondered and bowed her head,
    And sat as still as a statue of stone;
Her heart was troubled yet comforted,
Remembering what the Angel had said
    Of an endless reign and of David's throne.

186 HENRY WADSWORTH LONGFELLOW (1807–1882)

Then the Kings rode out of the city gate,
  With a clatter of hoofs in proud array;
But they went not back to Herod the Great
For they knew his malice and feared his hate,
  And returned to their homes by another way.

❧ To the Children

from *STRUWWELPETER*

When the children have been good,
That is, be it understood,
Good at meal-times, good at play,
Good all night and good all day, —
They shall have the pretty things
Merry Christmas always brings.
Naughty, romping girls and boys
Tear their clothes and make a noise,
Spoil their pinafores and frocks,
And deserve no Christmas-box.
Such as these shall never look
At this pretty Picture-Book.

❧ To-morrow Shall Be
My Dancing Day

To-morrow shall be my dancing day:
  I would my true love did so chance
To see the legend of my play,
  To call my true love to my dance:

  Sing O my love, O my love, my love, my love;
  This have I done for my true love.

Then was I born of a virgin pure,
  Of her I took fleshly substance;
Thus was I knit to man's nature,
  To call my true love to my dance:

In a manger laid and wrapped I was,
  So very poor, this was my chance,
Betwixt an ox and a silly poor ass,
  To call my true love to my dance:

Then afterwards baptized I was;
  The Holy Ghost on me did glance,
My Father's voice heard from above,
  To call my true love to my dance:

  Sing O my love, O my love, my love, my love;
  This have I done for my true love.

❧ The True Christmas

So stick up *Ivie* and the *Bays,*
And then restore the *heathen* ways.
Green will remind you of the spring,
Though this great day denies the thing.
And mortifies the Earth and all
But your wild *Revels,* and loose *Hall.*
Could you wear *Flow'rs,* and *Roses* strow
Blushing upon your breasts *warm Snow,*
That very *dress* your lightness will
Rebuke, and wither at the Ill.
The brightness of this day we owe
Not unto *Music, Masque* nor *Showe:*
Nor gallant *furniture,* nor *Plate;*
But to the *Manger's* mean Estate.
His *life* while here, as well as *birth,*
Was but a check to *pomp* and *mirth;*
And all mans *greatness* you may see
Condemn'd by his *humility.*

   Then leave your open *house* and *noise,*
To welcom him with *holy Joys,*
And the poor *Shepherd's* watchfulness:
Whom *light* and *hymns* from Heav'n did bless.
What you *abound* with, cast abroad
To those that *want,* and ease your loade.

Who empties thus, will bring more in;
But riot is both *loss* and *Sin*.
Dress finely what comes not in sight,
And then you keep your *Christmas* right.

❧ Twelfth Night: or, King and Queen

Now, now the mirth comes
  With the cake full of plums,
Where bean's the king of the sport here;
  Beside we must know,
  The pea also
Must revel, as queen, in the court here.

  Begin then to choose,
  This night as ye use,
Who shall for the present delight here,
  Be a king by the lot,
  And who shall not
Be Twelfth-day queen for the night here.

  Which known, let us make
  Joy-sops with the cake;
And let not a man then be seen here,
  Who unurg'd will not drink
  To the base from the brink
A health to the king and queen here.

  Next crown a bowl full
  With gentle lamb's wool:
Add sugar, nutmeg, and ginger,

stanza continues

ROBERT HERRICK (1591–1674)

With store of ale too;
   And thus ye must do
To make the wassail a swinger.

   Give then to the king
   And queen wassailing:
And though with ale ye be whet here,
   Yet part from hence
   As free from offence
As when ye innocent met here.

ROBERT HERRICK (1591–1674)

❧ The Twelve Days of Christmas

On the first day of Christmas
  my true love sent to me:
A Partridge in a pear tree.

On the second day of Christmas
  my true love sent to me:
Two turtle doves
And a Partridge in a pear tree.

On the third day of Christmas
  my true love sent to me:
Three French Hens,
Two turtle doves
And a Partridge in a pear tree.

On the fourth day of Christmas
  my true love sent to me:
Four calling birds,
Three French Hens,
Two turtle doves
And a Partridge in a pear tree.

On the fifth day of Christmas
  my true love sent to me:
Five golden rings,

stanza continues

TRADITIONAL CAROL

Four calling birds,
Three French Hens,
Two turtle doves
And a Partridge in a pear tree.

On the sixth day of Christmas
  my true love sent to me:
Six geese a laying,
Five golden rings,
Four calling birds,
Three French Hens,
Two turtle doves
And a Partridge in a pear tree.

On the seventh day of Christmas
  my true love sent to me:
Seven swans a swimming,
Six geese a laying,
Five golden rings,
Four calling birds,
Three French Hens,
Two turtle doves
And a Partridge in a pear tree.

On the eighth day of Christmas
  my true love sent to me:
Eight maids a milking,

stanza continues

Seven swans a swimming,
Six geese a laying,
Five golden rings,
Four calling birds,
Three French Hens,
Two turtle doves
And a Partridge in a pear tree.

On the ninth day of Christmas
    my true love sent to me:
Nine ladies dancing,
Eight maids a milking,
Seven swans a swimming,
Six geese a laying,
Five golden rings,
Four calling birds,
Three French Hens,
Two turtle doves
And a Partridge in a pear tree.

On the tenth day of Christmas
    my true love sent to me:
Ten lords a leaping,
Nine ladies dancing,
Eight maids a milking,
Seven swans a swimming,
Six geese a laying,

stanza continues

TRADITIONAL CAROL

Five golden rings,
Four calling birds,
Three French Hens,
Two turtle doves
And a Partridge in a pear tree.

On the eleventh day of Christmas
   my true love sent to me:
Eleven pipers piping,
Ten lords a leaping,
Nine ladies dancing,
Eight maids a milking,
Seven swans a swimming,
Six geese a laying,
Five golden rings,
Four calling birds,
Three French Hens,
Two turtle doves
And a Partridge in a pear tree.

On the twelfth day of Christmas
   my true love sent to me:
Twelve drummers drumming,
Eleven pipers piping,
Ten lords a leaping,
Nine ladies dancing,
Eight maids a milking,

stanza continues

Seven swans a swimming,
Six geese a laying,
Five golden rings,
Four calling birds,
Three French Hens,
Two turtle doves
And a Partridge in a pear tree.

Upon Christ His Birth

Strange news! a city full? will none give way
To lodge a guest that comes not every day?
No inn, nor tavern void? yet I descry
One empty place alone, where we may lie:
In too much fullness is some want: but where?
Men's empty hearts: let's ask for lodging there.
But if they not admit us, then we'll say
Their hearts, as well as inns, are made of clay.

SIR JOHN SUCKLING (1609–1642)

❧ A Visit from St. Nicholas

'Twas the night before Christmas, when all through
   the house
Not a creature was stirring, not even a mouse;
The stockings were hung by the chimney with care,
In hopes that St. Nicholas soon would be there;

The children were nestled all snug in their beds,
While visions of sugar-plums danced through
   their heads;
And Mamma in her 'kerchief, and I in my cap,
Had just settled our brains for a long winter's nap,

When out on the lawn there arose such a clatter,
I sprang from my bed to see what was the matter.
Away to the window I flew like a flash,
Tore open the shutters and threw up the sash.

The moon on the breast of the new-fallen snow
Gave a lustre of mid-day to objects below,
When, what to my wondering eyes did appear,
But a miniature sleigh, and eight tiny rein-deer,

With a little old driver so lively and quick,
I knew in a moment he must be St. Nick.

stanza continues

More rapid than eagles his coursers they came,
And he whistled, and shouted, and called them
  by name:

"Now, Dasher! now, Dancer! now, Prancer and
  Vixen!
On, Comet! on, Cupid! on, Donder and Blixen!
To the top of the porch! to the top of the wall!
Now dash away! dash away! dash away, all!"

As leaves that before the wild hurricane fly,
When they meet with an obstacle, mount to the sky,
So up to the house-top the coursers they flew,
With the sleigh full of toys, and St. Nicholas too—

And then in a twinkling, I heard on the roof
The prancing and pawing of each little hoof.
As I drew in my head, and was turning around,
Down the chimney St. Nicholas came with a bound.

He was dressed all in fur, from his head to his foot,
And his clothes were all tarnished with ashes and
  soot;
A bundle of toys he had flung on his back,
And he looked like a peddler just opening his pack.

continues

CLEMENT CLARKE MOORE (1779–1863)   201

His eyes—how they twinkled! his dimples, how
    merry!
His cheeks were like roses, his nose like a cherry!
His droll little mouth was drawn up like a bow,
And the beard on his chin was as white as the snow;

The stump of a pipe he held tight in his teeth,
And the smoke it encircled his head like a wreath;
He had a broad face and a round little belly
That shook when he laughed, like a bowl full of jelly.

He was chubby and plump, a right jolly old elf,
And I laughed when I saw him in spite of myself;
A wink of his eye and a twist of his head
Soon gave me to know I had nothing to dread;

He spoke not a word, but went straight to his work,
And filled all the stockings; then turned with a jerk,
And laying his finger aside of his nose,
And giving a nod, up the chimney he rose.

He sprang to his sleigh, to his team gave a whistle,
And away they all flew like the down of a thistle.
But I heard him exclaim ere he drove out of sight—

"HAPPY CHRISTMAS TO ALL
AND TO ALL A GOOD NIGHT!"

❧ Wassail, Wassail

Wassail, Wassail, all over the town!
Our toast it is white, and our ale it is brown,
Our bowl it is made of the white maple tree;
With the wassailing bowl we'll drink to thee.

So here is to Cherry and to his right cheek,
Pray God send our master a good piece of beef,
And a good piece of beef that may we all see;
With the wassailing bowl we'll drink to thee.

And here is to Dobbin and to his right eye,
Pray God send our master a good Christmas pie,
And a good Christmas pie that may we all see;
With our wassailing bowl we'll drink to thee.

So here is to Broad May and to her broad horn,
May God send our master a good crop of corn,
And a good crop of corn that may we all see;
With the wassailing bowl we'll drink to thee.

And here is to Fillpail and to her left ear,
Pray God send out master a happy New Year,
And a happy New Year as e'er he did see;
With our wassailing bowl we'll drink to thee.

continues

ANONYMOUS

And here is to Colly and to her long tail,
Pray God send our master he never may fail
A bowl of strong beer; I pray you draw near,
And our jolly wassail it's then you shall hear.

Come, butler, come fill us a bowl of the best,
Then we hope that your soul in heaven may rest;
But if you do draw us a bowl of the small,
Then down shall go butler, bowl and all.

Then here's to the maid in the lily white smock,
Who tripped to the door and slipped back the lock!
Who tripped to the door and pulled back the pin,
For to let these jolly wassailers in.

ANONYMOUS

❧ We Three Kings

We three kings of Orient are;
Bearing gifts we traverse afar
Field and fountain, moor and mountain,
Following yonder star:

O star of wonder, star of night,
Star with royal beauty bright,
Westward leading, still proceeding,
Guide us to thy perfect light.

Melchior.
Born a king on Bethlehem plain,
Gold I bring, to crown him again —
King for ever, ceasing never,
Over us all to reign:

Gaspar.
Frankincense to offer have I;
Incense owns a Deity nigh:
Prayer and praising, all men raising,
Worship him, God most high:

Balthazar.
Myrrh is mine; its bitter perfume
Breathes a life of gathering gloom;

stanza continues

Sorrowing, sighing, bleeding, dying,
Sealed in the stone-cold tomb:

   All.
Glorious now, behold him arise,
King, and God, and sacrifice!
Heaven sings alleluya,
Alleluya the earth replies:

   O star of wonder, star of night,
   Star with royal beauty bright,
   Westward leading, still proceeding,
   Guide us to thy perfect light.

❧ We Wish You a Merry Christmas

We wish you a Merry Christmas,
We wish you a Merry Christmas,
We wish you a Merry Christmas
And a Happy New Year!

Glad tidings we bring
To you and your kin.
We wish you a Merry Christmas,
And a Happy New Year.

Oh, bring us some Christmas pudding,
Oh, bring us some Christmas pudding,
Oh, bring us some Christmas pudding
And a glass of good cheer!

We won't go until we get some,
We won't go until we get some,
We won't go until we get some
So bring it right here!

We wish you a Merry Christmas,
We wish you a Merry Christmas,
We wish you a Merry Christmas
And a Happy New Year!

❧ What Child Is This?

What child is this, Who, laid to rest, on Mary's lap
  is sleeping?
Whom angels greet with anthems sweet, while
  shepherds watch are keeping?
This, this is Christ the King, whom shepherds
  guard and angels sing:
Haste, haste to bring Him laud, the Babe, the Son
  of Mary.

Why lies He in such mean estate where ox and ass
  are feeding?
Good Christian, fear: for sinners here the silent
  Word is pleading.
This, this is Christ the King, whom shepherds
  guard and angels sing:
This, this is Christ the King, the Babe, the Son
  of Mary.

So bring Him incense, gold and myrrh, come,
  peasant, king to own Him;
The King of kings salvation brings, let loving hearts
  enthrone him.

stanza continues

Raise, raise the Song on high, the Virgin sings
  her lullaby:
Joy, joy for Christ is born, the Babe, the Son
  of Mary.

∾ Whence Comes This Rush of Wings?

Whence comes this rush of wings afar,
Following straight the Noël star?
Birds from the woods in wondrous flight,
Bethlehem seek this Holy Night.

"Tell us, ye birds, why come ye here,
Into this stable, poor and drear?"
"Hast'ning we seek the new-born King,
And all our sweetest music bring."

Hark! how the greenfinch bears his part,
Philomel, too, with tender heart,
Chants from her leafy dark retreat,
Re, mi, fa, sol, in accents sweet.

Angels and shepherds, birds of the sky,
Come where the Son of God doth lie;
Christ on earth with man doth dwell,
Join in the shout, "Noël, Noël!"

Winter

A wrinkled, crabbed man they picture thee,
  Old Winter, with a ragged beard as grey
As the long moss upon the apple-tree;
Blue lipt, an ice-drop at thy sharp blue nose;
  Close muffled up, and on thy dreary way,
Plodding alone through sleet and drifting snows.

They should have drawn thee by the high-
    heapt hearth,
  Old Winter! seated in thy great armed chair,
Watching the children at their Christmas mirth,
  Or circled by them, as thy lips declare
Some merry jest, or tale of murder dire,
  Or troubled spirit that disturbs the night,
Pausing at times to rouse the mouldering fire,
  Or taste the old October brown and bright.

❧ Winter Time

Late lies the wintry sun abed,
  A frosty, fiery sleepy-head;
Blinks but an hour or two; and then,
  A blood red orange, sets again.

Before the stars have left the skies,
  At morning in the dark I rise;
And shivering in my nakedness,
  By the cold candle, bathe and dress.

Close by the jolly fire I sit
  To warm my frozen bones a bit;
Or with a reindeer-sled, explore
  The colder countries round the door.

When to go out, my nurse doth wrap
  Me in my comforter and cap,
The cold wind burns my face, and blows
  Its frosty pepper up my nose.

Black are my steps on silver sod;
  Thick blows my frosty breath abroad;
And tree and house, and hill and lake,
  Are frosted like a wedding-cake.

❧ Yule Log

Come, bring with a noise,
My merrie, merrie boys,
The Christmas Log to the firing;
While my good Dame, she
Bids ye all be free;
And drink to your hearts' desiring.

With the last year's brand
Light the new block, and
For good successe in his spending,
On your Psaltries play,
That sweet luck may
Come while the log is a-tinding.

Drink now the strong Beere,
Cut the white loafe here,
The while the meat is a-shredding;
For the rare Mince-Pie
And the Plums stand by
To fill the paste that's a-kneading.

Index of Authors

Index of First Lines

INDEX OF FIRST LINES   221

Acknowledgments